DIRECTORY OF THEATRE RESOURCES
A guide to research collections
and information services

Compiled by Diana Howard, BA, FLA
Principal Librarian
Reference and Information Services
London Borough of Richmond upon Thames

Second Edition 1986

The Library Association
Information Services Group
and
The Society for Theatre Research

First edition published by the Arts Council of Great Britain in 1980 as Directory of Theatre Research and Information Resources in the United Kingdom

ISBN 0 946347 08 5

INTRODUCTION

This survey of theatre research resources and information services was carried out during 1985/86 to provide information to the Working Party on Library Provision for Theatre Research which was set up by the Library Association's Information Services Group (formerly R.S.I.S.), and funded by the Library Association.

The questionnaires returned by the organisations surveyed form the basis of the entries in this directory which, in effect, is the second edition of the *Directory of Theatre Research and Information Resources in the United Kingdom* published by the Arts Council of Great Britain in 1980.

The directory is divided into two parts —

Part One comprises a directory of public and private collections open to the public either freely or by subscription, the majority providing formal library services.

Part Two contains entries for those societies and associations serving the theatre which provide information services. It is not a comprehensive listing of theatre organisations.

As the Working Party's report shows the scene is changing very rapidly, and long established institutions are either moving, amalgamating, or regrettably, through lack of adequate funding, closing. The publishers would be most grateful if organisations could keep them informed of such changes, and also of any major acquisitions added to their collections.

Diana Howard

PART ONE

1–256

COLLECTIONS OF THEATRE MATERIAL IN LIBRARIES, MUSEUMS AND RECORD OFFICES

Arrangement

Collections are arranged under the name of the city or town in which they are situated.

The Index of Collections gives the number of the entry of those collections whose names do not indicate their location.

PUBLIC COLLECTIONS

PUBLIC LIBRARIES

Public libraries, in the main, date from the final decades of the nineteenth century. They are administered by the counties and metropolitan cities in the regions and by the boroughs in Greater London; this has led to a wide range of policies, standards and financial provision.

Each authority's Libraries Department — usually under the control of either the Education Committee, Amenities Committee or Leisure and Recreation Committee — administers a number of libraries of varying size. The most usual pattern is for main libraries, with lending, reference and local studies departments, to be located in the principal town or towns of the area, while the outer areas are served by branch or mobile libraries.

The public library provides the major resource for students up to the age of eighteen, and for growing numbers of adult education students.

Lending Libraries:

The stock will cover all but the most obscure subjects, and will range in level from the elementary and introductory work to the advanced monograph. The theatre arts are usually well represented, but are scattered due to the arrangement of the Dewey Classification, performance being in 792, play-texts and criticism in the 800s, biography at 920 and so on.

Borrowing material: books, and audio-visual materials are loaned to anyone who can produce a current library ticket. These are available to people who either live, work or study in the local authority area. The loan of books is free of charge, but there may be a fee payable on videos, recordings etc.

Once tickets have been obtained they may be used in most public libraries.

The Inter-Library Loan Service enables libraries to borrow requested items which are not in their own stock and which are available for loan in another public collection. This service is backed up by the British Library's loan services, and applies to books, play-sets and periodical articles.

The main disadvantage for the practitioner of the theatre arts is the question of availability of specific material on demand. This is usually a matter of chance and 'reservations' may take anything from a few days to a considerable number of weeks to arrive.

Reference Libraries:

The stock will include general and subject encyclopaedias and dictionaries plus a range of standard works on most broad subject fields.

Tickets are not required, the material and facilities being available to anyone who wishes to make use of them. Desks are normally available for study but the accommodation provided ranges from approximately 20 to 200 seats depending on the size of the building and the population served. Subject to copyright, photocopying facilities are provided in the majority of libraries.

Central Reference Libraries in most authorities will stock files of such works as *Who's who in the Theatre, London Theatre Record, Plays and Players, Play Index* and standard works such as the *Oxford Companion to the Theatre, McGraw-Hill Encyclopedia of Drama,* and works on individual periods and types of performance.

It should also be remembered that general works such as the newspaper colour supplements include material on the performing arts and indexes such as the *British Humanities Index* make their contents accessible.

Local Studies Collections:

These collections may be housed in separate departments or form part of the stock of the Reference Library. They will include files of the local newspapers which often provide the main or only source of information on places of entertainment in the area.

Although many libraries have collected 18th and 19th century material there is a considerable lack of early 20th century items. There is an increasing awareness of the responsibility of local collections to preserve the records of their local places of entertainment and a number have already come to agreements with local theatres to be repositories for their archives.

Many local studies librarians will assist with research but this is subject to staff availability and will not extend to other public collections. Enquiries may be made by letter, telephone or personal visit. It is always advisable to make an appointment.

Record Libraries and Drama and Play Departments:

In recent years these departments have been notable casualties of the cuts in finance, and long-playing records are giving way to cassettes and, in the near future, to compact discs. Besides music there are good recordings of plays available. There may be a charge.

Drama and Play Libraries are usually found in County Libraries, and will contain collections of playsets. (In non-county libraries these are available through the Lending Library.) Many libraries will be members of the British Theatre Association and will be able to borrow plays from their collection.

MUSEUMS

No museum has adequate space to display all their material, and all have considerable quantities of material in strong rooms and basements. It is therefore advisable to contact the keeper/curator to discover what items are not on view and how to gain access to them. However, this facility will normally be available only to serious researchers.

RECORD OFFICES

The archive collections housed in the county record offices contain registers, papers and reports, minutes and miscellaneous material on the institutions for which their governing body is or was responsible.

The Public Record Office and the county record offices contain material on the theatres, music halls and other places of entertainments which was collected to enable the officials to carry out the tasks of licensing and fire safety. Much valuable information is contained in correspondence and evidence presented to the licensing authorities by members of the public and by applicants' competitors, who were protesting about the granting of a new licence or the renewal of an old one.

Many collections also contain family and business papers deposited with them. In this directory county record offices are listed under the town in which they are located — usually the county town.

POLYTECHNICS, COLLEGES OF HIGHER EDUCATION

Colleges submitting returns have been included in the directory, in addition however there are a number of colleges teaching drama and theatre arts courses whose libraries contain good general collections on theatre.

The majority of these libraries are available to the public for reference purposes and they may be situated in areas away from large central reference libraries which makes their collection of particular value in their locality.

For a list of these colleges see DATEC *directory of drama courses in higher education* (British Theatre Institute).

LIMITED ACCESS COLLECTIONS

These collections include those in the libraries of universities, the libraries of membership organisations such as those of societies, associations and clubs, and private collections whether belonging to an individual or commercial organisation.

The collections vary from the near comprehensive to the eccentric. Admission is granted at the discretion of the staff or owner, and may be a formality or a grudgingly given favour, or be accompanied with a request for substantial fees.

Personal collections held by private individuals have not been included in this directory. The Society for Theatre Research is compiling a register of these collections and may be contacted for information.

Prospective users of these collections are advised to write for permission to see them, explaining the purpose of their studies and why it is necessary to see the particular material held. An accompanying letter of introduction may also assist the applicant.

National Libraries:

Under the Copyright Act, 1911 it is necessary for authors to deposit a copy of each of their books, pamphlets etc. with the British Library. These copies are available to readers holding tickets in the British Library Reference Division, Bloomsbury.

Five other libraries have the right to claim deposit copies, these are the Libraries of the University of Cambridge, the University of Oxford (the Bodleian), the National Library of Scotland, the National Library of Wales and the Library of Trinity College, Dublin.

Archives of Theatres:

A number of theatre archives have recently been deposited in public collections, however a number of theatres are recognising the importance of their own archives and are employing archivists to maintain them.

These collections within theatres have been excluded except for two collections of long standing — at Covent Garden and the Bristol Old Vic. Both the Theatre Royal, Drury Lane and the Royal Exchange Theatre Manchester are maintaining collections, as is the Victoria Theatre, Stoke on Trent.

It is hoped eventually to survey other theatres to find out their plans for either maintaining their own collections or depositing them on a formal basis.

Researchers wishing to contact theatres should refer to the *British Theatre Directory* and the *British Alternative Theatre Directory,* both published by John Offord Publications.

ABERDEEN
1   ABERDEEN CITY LIBRARY

Rosemount Viaduct, Aberdeen, Scotland   (0224) 28991

Contact	Peter Grant, City Librarian
Admission	Unrestricted
Hours	Monday–Friday 9–9, Saturday 9–5
Contents	The Local Collection has a substantial amount of information on the theatrical history of Aberdeen, including 67 playbills bound in volumes and 750 single items, covering Her Majesty's Theatre, 1886–1902, His Majesty's Theatre 1909–23, 1933 to date, Beech Pavilion (Harry Gordon) 1924–38, plus a few items relating to Tivoli Theatre. Also background information in the shape of published works, newscuttings etc.

ABERDEEN
2   ABERDEEN COLLEGE OF EDUCATION, Library

Hilton Place, Aberdeen AB9 1FA   (0224) 42341

Contact	C. Smith-Burnett
Admission	For reference to any member of public
Hours	Term time: Monday–Friday 9–9.30, Saturday 9.30–12.30, Vacations: Monday–Friday 9–5
Contents	General collection of texts, criticism, books on theatre, plus drama records — relevant to the needs of drama and theatre studies students.

ABERYSTWYTH
3A   NATIONAL LIBRARY OF WALES

Aberystwyth, Dyfed SY23 3BU   (0970) 3816–9

Contact	The Librarian
Admission	By readers ticket; day tickets available
Hours	Monday–Friday 9.30–6, Saturday 9.30–5
Contents	National library; as a copyright library it is entitled to receive a copy of each title published. Arrangement by Library of Congress classification.

ABERYSTWYTH

3B UNIVERSITY COLLEGE OF WALES, ABERSTWYTH.
The Hugh Owen Library

Penglais, Aberystwyth, Dyfed SY23 3DZ (0970) 3111 Ext. 3006

Telex 35181

Admission Reference use only for those unconnected with College

Hours Term time: Monday–Friday 9–10, Saturday 9–1
Vacations: Monday–Friday 9–5.30
Closed for a week at Christmas and Easter and for the New Year and August Bank Holidays

Contents Several thousand works on theatre and drama, play texts and 17 periodicals on drama and theatre.

ALSAGER

4 CREWE & ALSAGER COLLEGE OF HIGHER EDUCATION.
Dr Annie Parkes Library

Alsager, Stoke on Trent ST7 2HL (09363) 3231

Admission All material available for reference. Local residents may register as external borrowers. Books available on inter-library loan.

Hours Term time: Monday–Thursday 9–8, Friday 9–5, Saturday 10–noon. Vacations: Monday–Friday 9–5

Contents Archive of North West Playwrights Co-operative. Ms plays from National Playwrights Conference, Eugene O'Neill Theatre Center U.S.A. 6,000 books about theatre and drama, 510 playsets, 20 periodicals with backfiles.

AYLESBURY

5 BUCKINGHAMSHIRE RECORD OFFICE

County Hall, Aylesbury, Buckinghamshire HP20 1UA (0296) 5000 Ext. 586

Contact H. A. Hanley, County Archivist

Admission Unrestricted, but advance booking of a seat is advisable

Hours Tuesday–Fri 9–5.15 (Early closing Friday 4.45)

Contents Usual licensing and property records. Abstract of title for the Theatre Royal, Margate (Grubb coll.D/42/0/23). Letter from Lady Elizabeth Lee to her neice, 11 July 1723 referring to theatrical performance given by Mr Grenville (Lee papers D/LE/A/4/11). Scrapbook containing theatre etc. programmes, London professional companies and amateur performances in the Barnham, Bucks., area c.1880–1900 (D/X 542). Business correspondence re: Leatherface Ltd., theatrical company, 1916–1924 (Freemantle MSS D/FR/A/39).

Note All postal enquiries should be accompanied by a stamped and addressed envelope.

BATH

6 BATH REFERENCE LIBRARY

18 Queen Square, Bath BA1 2HP   (0225) 28144

Contact	Mrs M. Joyce, Reference Librarian
Admission	Restricted to bona fide students. Application to the Reference Librarian
Hours	Monday–Friday 9.30–7.30, Saturday 9.30–5
Contents	Large collection relating to the Theatre Royal, Bath, including 6,050 playbills and programmes for 1772–1891 and c.500 press notices for 1920s–1971.

BEDFORD

7 BEDFORD COUNTY RECORD OFFICE

County Hall, Bedford MK42 9AP   (0234) 63222 Ext. 277

Contact	Miss P. L. Bell, County Archivist
Admission	Unrestricted
Hours	Monday–Friday 9–1, 2–5
Contents	Licensing and property records. Also documents, playbills, cuttings, reminiscences etc. relating to Bedfordshire theatres active between the 17th and 20th centuries. (Copies of many of the typed catalogues are available for consultation at the National Register of Archives, London.)

BEDFORD

8 BEDFORD MUSEUM

Castle Lane, Bedford   (0234) 53323

Contact	John Turner, Curator
Hours	Tuesday–Saturday 11–5; Sundays and Bank Holiday Mondays 2–5. Closed every Monday except Bank Holiday Monday.
Contents	A few late 18th century playbills; about a dozen 1860s Biggleswade theatre playbills.

BIRKENHEAD

9 WIRRAL ARCHIVES SERVICE

Birkenhead Reference Library, Borough Road, Birkenhead, Merseyside
                                                        (051) 652 6106–8

Contacts	D. N. Thompson, Archivist
	Miss C. E. Bidston, Local History Librarian
Hours	Monday, Tuesday, Thursday, Friday 10–8. Saturday 10–1, 2–8, Closed Wednesday
Contents	Argyle Theatre of Varieties, Birkenhead: (Opened 1867, closed

after bomb damage Sept. 1940.) A collection of c.570 playbills covering the years 1889–1931, but most complete for the years 1890–1915. Filed in chronological order.

BIRMINGHAM

10 BIRMINGHAM CENTRAL LIBRARY

Chamberlain Square, Birmingham B3 3HQ   (021) 235 4511

Hours   Monday–Friday 9–8, Saturday 9–5

Theatre material is located in four Reference Library departments

Fine Arts Department

Contact   Derek Fontaine   (021) 235 3390

Contents   General theatre history, theatrical biography, music hall, pantomime, puppetry, mime, ballet and modern dance, in addition to the arts of stage production, design and lighting, costume design and makeup. Special collections include the John Ash Collection of printed books, manuscripts and photographs concerning the Oberammergau Passion Play; New York Theatre 1919–1961; and 26,000 photographs from the Vandamm Collection (on microfiche).

Language and Literature Department

contains the reference collection of play texts, dramatic history and criticism, and incorporates:

The Birmingham Shakespeare Library

Contact   Niky Rathbone   (021) 235 4227

Contents   41,000 volumes of Shakespeare editions and criticism in over 90 languages. Main holdings are in English, followed by French and German. The Library includes the first four folios and some early quartos; a comprehensive collection of 17th–20th century editions. Newscuttings: over 200 volumes of newscuttings, especially reviews. Playbills: about 15,000 18th and 19th century playbills. Illustrations: the H. R. Forrest, James Turner and Pearson Illustrations Collections mainly 18th and 19th century. The Bennett Collection on Covent Garden from 1630–1922. Garrick's Jubilee and 1864 Tercentenary collections. There are also posters, programmes and photographs of over 6,000 British and foreign stage and film productions. About 2,000 music scores, 200 records, some prompt books and transcripts of BBC and ITV scripts.

Note   *Theatrephile* Vol. 1, no. 2 March 1984. The Shakespeare Library, Birmingham, by Niky Rathbone.

Local Studies and Archives Department

Contact   Patrick Baird   (021) 235 4399

Contents   Birmingham theatre history, including an extensive collection of Birmingham Theatre Royal prompt books, mainly 19th century.

Birmingham Repertory Theatre archive, including prompt books, and photographs of productions are on permanent deposit.

Music Department

Contact	Malcolm Jones (021) 235 2614
Contents	Opera, musical history and a large collection of scores.
Indexes	Playbills partly indexed, newscuttings partly indexed. Indexes to programmes and photographs.
Catalogues	Microfiche and card, author and classified catalogues.
Published catalogues	Payne, W. *A Shakespeare Bibliography* 7 vols. 1971. *Catalogue of the Birmingham Collection.* 1918, supplement 1931.

BIRMINGHAM

11 UNIVERSITY OF BIRMINGHAM. Library

Special Collections Department, P.O. Box 363, Birmingham B15 2TT
(021) 472 1301 Ext. 2439

Telex	338160
Contact	Special Collections Librarian
Admission	Available to any bona fide research worker presenting letter of introduction.
Hours	Monday–Friday 9–5
Contents	Professor Allardyce Nicoll Collection of approximately 7,000 programmes relating to London theatres, 1870–1969, with card index to titles and playwrights. Collections of Bridgnorth playbills, 1882–4, Birmingham programmes 1795–1876, and 1920–70; playbills for the Haymarket Theatre, London, 1846–7. The Theatre Royal, Leamington Spa, Collection includes the papers of its proprietor Charles Watson Mill, plays in typescript, part-books, letters and documents relating to family and business matters during his tenure, which covered the years 1910–1934. Ruth Williams donation of Birmingham theatre programmes.

BLACKBURN

12 BLACKBURN CENTRAL LIBRARY

Town Hall Street, Blackburn, Lancashire BB2 1AH (0254) 661221

Contact	Blackburn District Librarian
Hours	Monday–Wednesday 9.30–8, Thursday–Friday 9.30–5, Saturday 9.30–4
Contents	Local History Section:– 60 playbills and programmes from 1787 to 1940s. Newspaper cuttings from 1900s to date. Music and Drama Library:– 360 play sets, 1,200 books of texts, histories and criticism.

BOURNEMOUTH
13   LANSDOWNE REFERENCE LIBRARY
Dorset County Library, Lansdowne, Bournemouth BH1 3DJ   (0202) 292021

Contact	Reference Library
Admission	By appointment as material is not housed in this building
Hours	Monday–Friday 9.30–7, Saturday 9–1
Contents	Programmes and playbills for Bournemouth theatres:– Grand Theatre 1895 and 1904; New Town Hall 1888–1895; Pavilion 1930–1973; Winter Gardens 1894–1974; Theatre Royal 1893–1931. Items are held between the above dates, the files are not complete.

BOURNEMOUTH
14   RUSSELL-COTES ART GALLERY AND MUSEUM
East Cliff, Bournemouth BA1 3AA   (0202) 21009

Contact	G. Teasdill, Curator
Admission	Available to bona fide students
Hours	(Research Room) Monday–Saturday 10.45–12, 3–4.30
Contents	Material relating mainly to Sir Henry Irving and the Lyceum Theatre, London, including 5 prompt books, programmes and playbills, paintings, drawings, photographs, business records and letters; also a few costumes and props.

BRADFORD
15   BOLLING HALL MUSEUM
Bowling Hall Road, Bradford, West Yorkshire BD4 7LP   (0274) 723057

Contact	Mrs Anthea Bickley, Keeper of History
Admission	Researchers by appointment
Hours	Tuesday–Sunday 10–5 (April–September 10–6)
Contents	Playbills and programmes relating to Bradford theatres — The Theatre Royal, Alhambra and St. George's Hall.
Indexes	General collection index only. Playbills not indexed.

BRADFORD
16   BRADFORD CENTRAL LIBRARY
Prince's Way, Bradford BD1 1NN   (0274) 33081

Contact	W. Davies, Librarian
Admission	Unrestricted
Hours	Monday–Friday 9–8, Saturday 9–5
Contents	Approximately 560 playbills and 250 programmes relating to local

theatres, including Records of Bradford Theatre Royal 1921–61, Bradford Playhouse 1919–1939, financial records of Alhambra Theatre 1921–1970. Detailed listing available.

BRIGHTON

17   BRIGHTON PUBLIC LIBRARY

Church Street, Brighton BN1 1UE   (0273) 691195 Ext. 25

Contact	The Reference Librarian
Admission	Unrestricted
Hours	Monday 10–7, Tuesday, Thursday & Friday 10–7, Saturday 10–4, Closed Wednesday
Contents	In the Local Collection, 5,000 playbills of Brighton theatres, 1820–1900, 1,000 programmes of the 1890s and 1,000 programmes of the local theatres 1920–30s. The Reference Library includes approximately 1,000 playbills of London theatres in the 19th century (Bloomfield Collection) and approximately 1,000 programmes.

BRISTOL

18   BRISTOL OLD VIC COMPANY

Theatre Royal, King Street, Bristol BS1 4ED   (0272) 277466

Contact	Rodney West, General Manager
Admission	Scholars are welcome to visit the theatre, by arrangement, to conduct their own research. It is not possible for the theatre to enter into any correspondence,
Contents	Scripts of plays performed recently, prompt copies, posters and programmes, certain show-tapes, a huge collection of costumes and furniture, press cutting books, architects' plans for the redevelopment around the Theatre Royal, and full records of the administration of the Bristol Old Vic. (Historical records are deposited with the Bristol City Record Office, q.v.)

BRISTOL

19   BRISTOL RECORD OFFICE

Council House, College Green, Bristol BS1 5TR   (0272) 26031 Ext. 441/2

Contact	City Archivist — Miss M. E. Williams, B.A.
Admission	Unrestricted
Hours	Monday–Thursday 8.45–4.45, Friday 8.45–4.15, Saturday 9–12 (by appointment only)
Contents	Theatre material consists of administrative, financial and professional records of the Theatre Royal, Bristol, and the Rapier Players, Bristol, including prompt books, programmes, photographs and press cuttings. The collection of playbills, which covers

drama, pantomime, ballet and opera, includes items referring to Grimaldi, Macready, Kean and Ellen Terry. Theatres featured include the Theatre Royal, Prince's, Athenaeum, Hippodrome Empire and Little Theatre, Bristol; theatres in Bath, Plymouth, Worcester, Portsmouth and Southsea; eleven 19th century London theatres.

Refs   8976–8982, 9307–9313, 9727, 17558, 26404, 31645

BRISTOL
20   BRISTOL REFERENCE LIBRARY
Avon County Library Headquarters, College Green, Bristol BS1 5TL
(0272) 276121

Contact   G. Langley, County Reference Librarian
Admission   Unrestricted, but advance notice is required if the enquirer wishes to consult valuable material.
Hours   Monday–Friday 9.30–8, Saturday 9.30–5
Contents   There is a substantial collection of playbills, programmes and ephemera relating to the history of the theatre in Bristol, plus some manuscript material. There is no catalogue.
Indexes   Indexes to Bristol playbills have been compiled by Kathleen Barker.

BRISTOL
21   UNIVERSITY OF BRISTOL. Theatre Collection
Department of Drama, The University, 29 Park Row, Bristol BS1 5LT
(0272) 24161 Ext. 654

Contact   Miss Ann Brooke Barnett, Keeper of the Theatre Collection
Admission   Readers' tickets can be made available to visitors on application in writing, or by telephone to the Keeper.
Hours   Monday–Friday 10–5
Contents   The contents of the collections are described in *University of Bristol Theatre Collection: a guide to readers (1972)*. It is a "working collection of graphic material illustrative of theatre history . . . . It contains some fine original source material . . . . Also photographic, supported by books . . . ."
It includes:–
Dr Richard Southern Collection, purchased in 1966. The Robinson Bequest of 18th and 19th century West Country playbills. The Landstone Bequest: A complete set of London theatre programmes of professional productions 1944–1969. The *Monuments Scenica,* and a portfolio of Appia designs. The Beerbohm Tree Collection: in particular relating to His Majesty's Theatre, comprising 325 costume designs, 245 prompt books, 230 agreements, rights and licences, 25 account

books and ledgers, 6 theatre plans and 64 books of press cuttings. The Beerbohm Tree correspondence was acquired in 1981. The Allan Tagg Collection of designs from the 1956 production of *Look Back in Anger* to the present day. The Eric Jones-Evans Collection of Theatrical Ephemera includes unique material connected with Sir Henry Iriving, Sir John Martin-Harvey, Bransby Williams and Fred Terry. The London Old Vic Archive has been deposited on indefinite loan. The Bristol Old Vic Archives are held.

Note   *Theatrephile*, Vol 1, no. 1, December 1983. The Bristol Theatre Collection, by Christopher Robinson.

BROMLEY

22 BROMLEY PUBLIC LIBRARIES. Anerley Branch Library

206d Anerley Road, London SE20   (01) 778 7457

Contact   The Branch Librarian

Hours   Monday 9.30–8, Tuesday, Wednesday & Friday 9.30–6, Saturday 9.30–5

Contents   Special collection on the Crystal Palace.

BROMLEY

23 BROMLEY PUBLIC LIBRARIES. Local History Collection

Central Library, High Street, Bromley, Kent BR1 1EX   (01) 460 9955

Telex   896712

Contact   Local Studies Library

Hours   Monday closed; Tuesday & Thursday 9.30–8; Wednesday & Friday 9.30–6; Saturday 9.30–5

Contents   Programmes from Bromley Little Theatre, 1935 onwards; (Bromley) New Theatre, 1947 onwards; Empire Theatre, Penge, 1941–9; Grand Theatre, Bromley (1903–1938); Churchill Theatre (1977–); and miscellaneous amateur programmes.

BURNLEY

24 BURNLEY DISTRICT LIBRARY

Grimshaw Street, Burnley, Lancashire BB11 2AS   (0282) 37115

Contact   Miss J. Siddall, Reference Librarian

Admission   Unrestricted

Hours   Monday, Wednesday, Thursday 9.30–7, Tuesday 9.30–1, Friday 9.30–5; Saturday 9.30–1, 2–4

Contents   c.50 programmes for the Palace and Victoria Theatres (20th century). Reports and correspondence on setting up a civic theatre 1946–1966. Visitors Book of Mrs Robinson, a Burnley theatrical landlady 1901–08. 30 photographs of local theatres.

BURNLEY

25 TOWNELEY HALL ART GALLERY AND MUSEUMS

Burnley, Lancashire BB11 3RQ   (0282) 24213

Contact	H. R. Rigg, Curator
Hours	Summer: Monday–Friday 10–5.30, Sunday 12–5.
	Winter: Monday–Friday 10–5.15, Sunday 12–5.
	Closed Saturdays throughout the year
Contents	9 playbills and programmes relating to local theatres.

BURY

26 BURY CENTRAL LIBRARY

Local History Collection, Manchester Road, Bury, Lancashire BL9 0DR
                                                        (061) 764 4110

Contact	Mrs Hirst, Reference Librarian
Admission	Unrestricted
Hours	Monday–Friday 9–7.30, Saturday 9–4.30
Contents	The collection includes information on various theatres in Bury, including Theatre Royal and Hippodrome, photographs, news cuttings, pamphlets. Most of the programmes related to entertainments provided by the Local Authority.

BURY ST. EDMUNDS

27 MOYSES HALL MUSEUM

Corn Hill, Bury St. Edmunds   (0284) 63233

Contact	Miss E. J. Owles, Curator
Admission	40p (children/OAPs half price)
Hours	Monday–Saturday 10–1, 2–5 (closes 4 pm November–February)
Contents	Lord Chamberlain's licence for *Charley's Aunt*. Silver admission tickets used by the original shareholders of the Theatre Royal in 1819. Theatre Royal poster of 1868 — Mademoiselle Beatrice's Comedy Drama Company — Schiller's *Mary Stuart*.

BURY ST. EDMUNDS

28 SUFFOLK RECORD OFFICE

Bury St. Edmunds Branch, Raingate Street, Bury St. Edmunds IP33 1RX
                                                   (0284) 63141 Ext. 384

Contact	R. Gwyn Thomas, Senior Assistant Archivist
Admission	Unrestricted
Hours	Monday–Thursday 9–5, Friday 9–4, Saturday 9–1, 2–5. Documents for use on Saturdays must be requested by 1 pm on Friday

Contents	Acc. 421 Correspondence of William Wilkins, architect and first proprietor of the theatre now known as the Theatre Royal, Bury St. Edmunds, and his son, with their solicitor James Borton, 1818–1846 (See Sybil Rosenfeld *William Wilkins and the Bury St. Edmunds Theatre, Theatre Notebook* XIII, p.20). D7/6/33 Appointment of new trustees of the Theatre Royal, 1846. E4/29/12 Deeds of site of the Theatre Royal, 1770–1820, with papers re: insurance of the theatres at Norwich, Colchester and Ipswich. D4/1 Entry Books of the Corporation. There are references to the Corporation's relations with the theatre from 1734 onwards. Acc. 1484 About 180 playbills, 1824–46. Acc. 2799 42 playbills, 1776–1802. Acc 2965 Posters, etc., 1966–72. Also pictorial material, particularly of restoration of the Theatre Royal during 1961–65. Files of the local newspaper, 1782 to date. Printed material on the history of the theatre.
Loan facilities	Loans to responsible organisations are considered for exhibition purposes.

BUXTON

29 BUXTON MUSEUM AND ART GALLERY

Terrace Road, Buxton, Derbyshire SK17 6DJ   (0298) 4658

Contact	M. J. Bishop
Hours	Tuesday–Friday 9.30–5.30, Saturday 9.30–5
Contents	Buxton playbills 1790s+ (especially 19th century). Buxton programmes, mainly early 20th century. Photographs, cuttings, ephemera for Buxton theatre history and the reinstatement of the Buxton Opera House and Buxton Festival. (McCoola Collection.)
Indexes	Simple name catalogue.
Published guide	*Theatre in the Hills,* by Ros McCoola, Caron Publications, 1984, largely based on research materials available in this collection.

CAERNARFON

30 GWYNEDD ARCHIVES SERVICE

Caernarfon Record Office, County Offices, Caernarfon, Gwynedd

(0286) 4121

Contact	Assistant County Archivist
Admission	Unrestricted
Hours	Monday, Tuesday, Thursday 9.30–5, Wednesday 9.30–7, Friday 9.30–4
Contents	Some playbills and programmes, plus a few photographs. Some letters relating to touring companies. Complete set of post–1930 licences for Caernarfon.

CAMBRIDGE
31A CAMBRIDGE CENTRAL LIBRARY
7 Lion Yard, Cambridge CB2 3QD   (0223) 65252

Contact	Local Studies Library
Admission	Unrestricted
Hours	Monday–Friday 9.30 5.30, Saturday 9–5
Contents	Books and unpublished dissertations — histories, reminiscences, plays, etc. Programmes — Arts, Festival and New Theatres. Playbills — Stourbridge Theatre 1791–1805; Theatre Royal, Barnwell 1806–1899. Newscuttings — 1958–. Newspapers indexed 1770–1984. Illustrations — engravings and photographs of buildings, performances etc. Play texts of plays originally produced in Cambridge or by local playwrights.

CAMBRIDGE
31B CAMBRIDGE UNIVERSITY LIBRARY
West Road, Cambridge CB3 9DR   (0223) 337733 Ext. 3000

Contact	The Deputy Librarian
Admission	On application
Hours	Monday–Friday 9–10 pm, Saturday 9–1
Contents	As a copyright library it has the right to receive a copy of all titles published. Large collection of 20th century Cambridge theatre programmes.

CAMBRIDGE
32 COUNTY RECORD OFFICE, CAMBRIDGE
Shire Hall, Castle Hill, Cambridge CB3 0AP   (0223) 317281

Contact	J. M. Farrar, County Archivist
Admission	Unrestricted
Hours	Monday–Thursday 9–5.15, Friday 9–4.15 (Tuesday late evening until 9 pm by appointment)
Contents	Programmes of New Theatre, Cambridge, 28–30 March 1901, 19–24 May 1902, 24 November 1930, 16 February 1931. (Refs: R58/2/1-2, 553/Z84). Sale of shares of Cambridge New Theatre Company, 1910 (Ref: 515/SP420). Licensing records: Minutes from 1896, files from c.1910 for the former Councils of Cambridgeshire and the Isle of Ely. Photograph of Wisbech theatre bill, 1782 (R75/30). Register of theatres and cinemas visited by John Cowell of Soham 1905–74 (Ref: R83/27). Accounts in connection with play of Holy Martyr St. George in Bassingbourn, 1511 (Ref: P11/5/2).

CANTERBURY

33 CANTERBURY CATHEDRAL, CITY AND DIOCESAN ARCHIVES

The Precincts, Canterbury, Kent CT1 2EG   (0227) 463510

Contact   Miss A. M. Oakley

Admission   By appointment

Contents   T. S. Eliot's *Murder in the Cathedral* — original acting copy with the author's notes; also photographs of the original production taken by Fisk-Moore, and sketches for the costumes. Texts of other plays commissioned by the Friends of Canterbury Cathedral. (Additional MSS 101–103.)

CANTERBURY

34 CANTERBURY LIBRARY

High Street, Canterbury, Kent CT1 2JF   (0227) 463608 and 69964

Contact   Mrs J. Adamson, Group Librarian

Hours   Monday, Tuesday, Friday 9.30–6, Wednesday, Thursday, Saturday 9.30–5

Contents   The A. E. Johnson Collection: This collection has not yet been catalogued but includes: Playbills and programmes for the Theatre Royal, local music halls and other centres from the Edwardian to the Mid-Twenties period. Typescript records of productions at the Theatre Royal (1861–1908) and at some other local venues. (Information collected from local newspapers.) Programmes of Marlowe Theatre productions from March 1967. 'Theatre in Canterbury': an exhibition of c.100 photographs and illustrations assembled in 1984. This illustrates Canterbury's theatrical history from Roman to present times and is kept as a permanent record.

CANTERBURY

35 THE UNIVERSITY OF KENT AT CANTERBURY. Library

Canterbury, Kent CT2 7NU   (0227) 66822

Librarian   W. J. Simpson

Contact   Stephen Holland, Assistant Librarian in charge of Special Collections

Admission   Material in Special Collections can be consulted by appointment Monday–Saturday 9–5

Contents   **The Frank Pettingell/Arthur Williams Collection**
A collection of several thousand printed texts and c.1300 manuscripts and typescripts originally assembled by the Victorian comedian Arthur Williams and later acquired by Frank Pettingell. The emphasis is firmly on 19th century material with some spillage into early and later periods. The collection is particularly rich in

mss relating to productions at the Britannia Theatre, Hoxton (c.400 mss). These often duplicate mss in the Lord Chamberlain's Collection, but are usually superior both in length and evidence of performance. The following authors are well represented in the mss collection (often though not always holograph): S. Atkyns (34 mss); D. Boucicault (10 mss, some unpublished); C. H. Hazlewood (172 mss); F. Marchant (21 mss); E. Newbound (22 mss); G. D. Pitt (109 mss); W. Seaman (37 mss); C. A. Somerset (22 mss); C. H. Stephenson (49 mss).

The original collection has been added to by the purchase of several hundred playbills, mostly from the London theatres, and by much textual material not in the collection, particularly about 600 printed texts, many used by the Victorian actor Marcus Elmore. As the collection was originally put together by Victorian actors, many of the texts bear the characteristics of a working collection with many marked copies and prompt copies being present.

Back up to the central textual collection is provided by (a) a growing collection of 19th century monographs on the theatre; (b) major fiche collections like the Playbills, prompt books, and actor's copies in the Theatre Museum; (c) 19th century theatrical periodicals on microfilm or hard copy. Titles acquired so far include: *Actors by Daylight* nos 1–48, 1838; *Dramatic Notes* 1879–88, 90–91; *Dramatic Register* 1853; *Era* 1867–1939; *Era Almanack and Annual* 1868–1919; *The Theatre* 1878–97; *Theatre Annual* 1884–8; *Theatrical Journal* 1839–60, 69–71; *Theatrical Observer and Daily Bills of the Play* 1821–44; *Theatrical Times* nos 1–62, 1846–7.

Other Drama Materials in the Library
The Special Collections Room houses all early editions of plays up to 1800, and much textual material of a later date relating to Renaissance drama from the library of John Crow. For this early period the Readex Microprint *'Three Centuries of Drama'* on microcard is our most important resource.

A small amount of related 19th century textual material not yet listed, from the John Crow Collection and the Joan Wake gift. c.350 19th century playbills/early programmes, uncatalogued. Late 18th/early 19th century collections, e.g. Inchbald's *British Theatre* 25 vols; Inchbald's Farces 7 vols; Bell's *British Theatre* (many volumes and singles from the 1776 ed. onwards, not yet sorted); Dodsley's *Old Plays* 12 vols. Also Collier's *Supplement and Old Plays,* a continuation of Dodsley's 6 vols; Farces, supplement to the British Theatre 4 vols. (Edinburgh 1786) etc. All pre–1800 editions of individual authors (selective 19th century editions). Includes some 17th century material, e.g. first two folio editions of Beaumont and Fletcher, much uncatalogued.

Miscellaneous items, e.g. memoirs, editions of Baker's Playhouse Companion, postcards of music hall performers, (c.60), a small number of 20th century theatre programmes etc.

Catalogues	Most material is listed in the main Author Catalogue; large quantities of material are so far uncatalogued. The Frank Pettingell/ Arthur Williams Collection has its own set of checklists. These are at present being amalgamated to form a single author sequence, with added entries for title, year of first performance, provenance etc. This new catalogue will eventually be microfilmed and published.
Microfilmed collections	We have issued one microfilm collection of the printed plays of Dion Boucicault. The University now has a contract with Harvester Press to have the whole Pettingell/Williams Collection microfilmed. Filming, initially of the manuscripts, will start in 1985.

CARDIFF

36 DRAMA ASSOCIATION OF WALES

1st Floor, Chapter Arts Centre, Market Road, Canton, Cardiff CF5 1OE

(0222) 43794

Contact	Betty Williams, Membership Services Officer
Admission	To members only, unless membership inappropriate
Hours	Monday–Friday 9.30–1, 2–5
Contents	Library of plays in English and Welsh, organised in the following sections: Full length plays in sets; Full length plays in single copies; One act plays in sets; One act plays in single copies; One act plays for women in sets; One act plays for women in single copies; Plays for children and young people; Religious plays; Musicals; Sketches; Monologues and play extracts; Pantomimes; Full length play collections; One act play collections.
Information service	All queries regarding any aspect of theatre are dealt with. Schools and training courses are held regularly. This is the only national organisation in Wales catering for the needs, not only of amateur groups, but also professional companies. Varying subscription rates and hiring charges.
Indexes	Catalogue being revised to produce author and title sequences and basic information on each work, i.e. date of publication/first performance.

CARDIFF

37 WELSH COLLEGE OF MUSIC AND DRAMA. Library

Castle Grounds, Cathays Park, Cardiff CF1 3ER

(0222) 42854

Contact	R. Welch
Admission	Reference use. Lending facilities granted at the discretion of the librarian
Hours	Term time: Monday–Thursday 10–5.30, Friday 10–4.30 Vacations: Monday–Friday 10–4.30 with closure

Contents   Biography, criticism, history and techniques of drama and theatre. Play texts and recordings.

CARLISLE

38 CUMBRIA RECORD OFFICE, CARLISLE

The Castle, Carlisle CA3 8UR   (0228) 23456 Ext. 316

Contact	B. C. Jones, County Archivist
Admission	Unrestricted
Hours	Monday–Friday 9–5
Contents	Carlisle theatres:

Bijou Theatre Posters (1867–9); Royal Lyceum ('Matchbox') Plan 1860; Star Music Hall Plan and playbills 1877–82; Her Majesty's Theatre, programmes, playbills, plans etc. 1874–1968; Palace Theatre Plans 1905; Proposed Arts Centre. File 1970.

Whitehaven:
Theatre Royal. Records including account book, inventories, posters, minute book, letterbook 1885–1916; Empire Theatre, title deeds.

Miscellaneous:
Payment to 'waits', Carlisle 1602–1619; Play prologues 17th century; Plays purchased by Lowther family of Whitehaven 17th century; Harrogate playbills (3) 1791; Posters and programmes 18th–19th centuries; Kemble's petition to stage plays 1808; Maryport playbills 1782–1809; Letters from travelling players offering to play near Maryport 1798–1809; Plays supplied by John Ware, printer and stationer of Whitehaven 1798–1810; Guide to theatrical apartments, Carlisle 19th century; MSS. Cumberland dialect plays 20th century.
List of holding available.

CHELMSFORD

39 ESSEX RECORD OFFICE

County Hall, Chelmsford CM1 1LX   (0245) 267222 Ext. 2104

Contact	Victor W. Gray, County Archivist
Admission	By appointment only
Hours	Monday 10–8.45, Tuesday–Thursday 9.15–5.15, Friday 9.15–4.15, closed Saturday
Contents	Printed sources: Aaron Hill, *King Henry the Fifth,* a tragedy (Pub. London 1723); Anon, *The C. . . . II Volunteer Corps: a farce* (Colchester 1804); *Essex Plays* Vols. I, III (Colchester 1932, 1935). A collection of dialect plays. H. B. Dudley, *The Woodman,* a comic opera, 1971. D. Ogbourne, *The Merry Midnight Mistake,* a comedy,

1765.

General histories printed in the *Essex Review* (based on thesis by W. A. Mepham): O. Tapper, 'The Other Stratford' (West Ham Library, 1962); 'The Theatre Royal, E.15'; P. Sherry, 'A Theatre in the Family' (Research Publishing Co., 1972); 'The Numm family and the Theatre Royal, Colchester'.

J. K. Melling, *Southend Playhouses from 1793* (Essex Countryside, 1969). *Theatre-Chelmsford* Autumn Nos. 1 and 2 (Chelmsford Theatre Association 1965, 1966); history of Chelmsford Theatres.

Also a few prints and photographs.

Manuscript sources: Miscellaneous collection of documents, including playbills, letters, licensing records, etc. relating to local theatres. Also Deeds including shares in Dukes Theatre, Dorset Gardens, 1662–1692.

Talfourd Collection, c.1809–52 (D/DU 754): includes correspondence with/from actors including Henry Irving; scripts of plays by T. N. Talfourd, F. Talfourd, and J. M. Madox.

Green Collection, 1864–1920 (D/DU 681), 5 vols. of scrapbooks including theatre programmes.

Periodical articles and thesis on various aspects of Essex theatre history.

CHELTENHAM
40   CHELTENHAM ART GALLERY AND MUSEUM

Clarence Street, Cheltenham GL50 3JT   (0242) 37431

Contact	Dr S. Blake
Admission	Researchers by appointment
Hours	Monday–Saturday 10–5.30
Contents	Collection of approximately 3400 theatre playbills dating from 1791–1920. Mainly for Cheltenham theatres, but a small number for other Gloucestershire towns, and Bath, Birmingham, Brighton, Cardiff, Ilfracombe, London, Portsmouth and Teignmouth.
Indexes	Chronological list only.

CHESTER
41   CHESHIRE RECORD OFFICE

The Castle, Chester, Chester CH1 2DN   (0244) 602574

Contact	Brian C. Redwood, County Archivist
Admission	Records can usually be consulted at a few moment's notice in the search room, but advance notice is helpful, particularly for Saturday visits.

Hours	Monday 9–9, Tuesday–Friday 9–5, Saturday 9–12.30
Contents	Licensing records in the Cheshire Quarter Sessions Order Books.

CHESTER

42   CHESTER LIBRARY

Northgate Street, Chester CH1 2EF   (0244) 312935

Contact	J. G. Fisher, Principal Librarian
Hours	Monday, Tuesday, Thursday, Friday 9.30–8, Wednesday 9.30–5, Saturday 9.30–1
Contents	A volume of music hall bills and other items relating to the Gateway Theatre, Chester.

CHESTERFIELD

43   CHESTERFIELD CENTRAL LIBRARY. Local Studies

New Beetwell Street, Chesterfield, Derbyshire S40 1QN   (0246) 209292

Contact	J. Lilley, Local Studies Librarian
Hours	Monday–Friday 9.30–7, Saturday 9.30–4
Contents	Theatre Royal Chesterfield — 4 theatre bills for 1800, 1802, 1811, 1821. Chesterfield Civic Theatre Collection:– Newcuttings, 5 vols, 1949 to date; Programmes 1949–84; Miscellaneous financial statements, wage sheets, box office receipts; Prompt copies of productions. G. W. Allen Collection:– Small collection of theatre posters printed by local printer who supplied over 100 theatres around the country, covering period c.1935–1957; included in this collection are bills for the Chesterfield Hippodrome Theatre 1940–c.1950s.
Indexes	Collections are not yet fully catalogued.

CHICHESTER

44   PALLANT HOUSE GALLERY

9 North Pallant, Chichester, West Sussex   (0243) 774557

Contact	David Coke
Hours	Tuesday–Saturday 10–5.30
Contents	The Chichester Festival Theatre Archive, 1961+ — programmes, scripts, photographs, newscuttings, ephemera. The Hussey Bequest — includes theatrical designs by Bakst, Benois and 'Motley'.
Catalogues	Hussey Bequest *The Walter Hussey Collection,* by Neil Colyer, 1981. £1.25.

CHICHESTER

45 WEST SUSSEX RECORD OFFICE

County Hall, Chichester, Sussex PO19 1RN   (0243) 777983

Contact   Mrs P. Gill, County Archivist
Admission   Unrestricted
Hours   Monday–Friday 9.15–12.30, 1.30–5
Contents   Catalogue of title deeds of Arundel Theatre, 1755–1826
               (MP.124). Title deeds of Chichester Theatre, 1669–1841. (Raper
               MSS 244–271). Microfilm of James Winston Ms. in the Houghton
               Library, Harvard University re. Sussex Theatres 1800–1803
               (MF9). Posters for concerts, theatre and music hall at Horsham
               1823–1920 (MP1508). See also: 'Sources of information on 18th
               and early 19th century Theatres in Sussex' in *Theatre Notebook*, Vol.
               XII, no. 2 (1958), pp.58–64.

COLCHESTER

46 COLCHESTER AND ESSEX MUSEUM

Museum Resource Centre, 14 Ryegate Road, Colchester, Kent CO1 1YG
                                                            (0206) 712481/2

Contact   Curator or Assistant Curator
Admission   Researchers by appointment
Hours   Monday–Friday 10–5
Contents   Reserve collection of a limited number of 19th century playbills
               relating to Colchester.

COLCHESTER

47 UNIVERSITY OF ESSEX. Library

P.O. Box 24, Colchester, Essex CO4 3UA   (0206) 862286

Contact   Librarian
Admission   On written application at the Librarian's discretion
Hours   Term time: Monday–Friday 9–10, Saturday 9–6, Sunday 2–7
               Vacations: Monday–Friday 9–5.30
Contents   The collections support the teaching of drama, at undergraduate
               and graduate level. Holdings relate mainly to English and
               American theatre and drama and includes major reference
               collection. The Library maintains an archival file of posters and
               programmes of all productions in the University Theatre.

COLNE

48 COLNE LIBRARY

Market Street, Colne, Lancashire   (0282) 865045
Contact   P. Wightman, Librarian

Hours	Monday, Wednesday 9.30–7, Thursday, Friday 9.30–5, Tuesday 9.30–12 noon, Saturday 9.30–4
Contents	1 MS of local pageant of church in Colne. 100 programmes of local societies. 3 theatre plans.

COVENTRY
49 COVENTRY REFERENCE LIBRARY
Coventry and Warwickshire Collection, 2nd Floor, Broadgate House, Coventry
(0203) 25555 Ext. 2768

Telex	31469
Contact	Andrew Mealey, Principal Librarian, Local Studies Division
Admission	Unrestricted
Hours	Monday–Thursday 8.30–5.45, Friday 8.30–4.45, Saturday 8.30–12.45
Contents	c.100 Coventry playbills from Victorian times. 28 vols. of 20th century programmes. c.500 photographs of early productions at the Belgrade Theatre. Collection also includes a few architects' plans, small newscuttings collections, and about 30 books relating to the medieval mystery plays, with special reference to Coventry.

COVENTRY
50 UNIVERSITY OF WARWICK. Central Library
Coventry CV4 7AL   (0203) 24011

Contact	Peter Larkin
Admission	External users may normally use the library for reference
Hours	Term time: Monday–Friday 9–7.30, Saturday 2–6 Vacations: Monday–Friday 9–5.30
Contents	History of European and North American theatre mainly for 19–20th centuries; popular theatre, music hall, cabaret, etc. Theory of directing and acting; stage designing and theatre design; dramatic theory; avant garde movements; Ancient and Oriental theatre; costume; movement and dance, (roughly 5,000 volumes and 91 periodicals, dead and current). Also some microfilm collections (i.e. Prompt Books, 16–19th century drama in English).

CROYDON
51 CROYDON PUBLIC LIBRARIES. Local History Library
Katharine Street, Croydon CR9 1ET   (01) 688 3627 Ext. 48

Contact	Stephen Roud, Local History Librarian
Hours	Monday 9.30–7, Tuesday–Friday 9.30–6, Saturday 9–5
Contents	Programmes, posters, magazine articles, ephemera and photo-

graphs on:–

Croydon Hippodrome (formerly Theatre Royal and Empire Theatre of Varieties), Croydon Theatre, Croydon Warehouse Theatre, Davis Theatre, Grand Theatre, Pembroke Theatre, Croydon & District Theatre Guild, Croydon Histrionic Society, Croydon Players, Croydon Repertory Theatre, Croydon Stagers Operatic Society, Shakespeare Memorial National Theatre (Croydon Branch), Croydon Community Theatre, Globe Theatre, Greyhound Theatre, Empire Theatre (formerly Palace of Varieties), Princess' Theatre, Royal Olympic Theatre, and Youth Theatre.

Indexes Index to theatres within the Local History Index giving basic details, date of opening, some performances, important events, etc.

CWMBRAN

52 GWENT COUNTY RECORD OFFICE

County Hall, Cwmbran, Gwent   (063 33) 67711

Contact Delwyn Tibbott, County Archivist

Admission Unrestricted

Hours Tuesday–Thursday 9.30–5, Friday 9.30–4

Contents 12 manuscripts and c.300 printed texts of plays, 14 playbills, 1 properties list, 22 letters and 11 prints relating to the Hendre Theatre, the amateur theatre company of the Rolls Family of the Hendre, Llangattock vibon Avell, later the Lords Llangattock. The material dates mostly from the first half of the 19th century. Correspondence includes letters from W. C. Macready to J. E. W. Rolls, and another item included in the collection is 'Recollections of the Scenic Effects of Covent Garden Theatre' dedicated to Macready, 1838.

DARLINGTON

53 BOROUGH OF DARLINGTON MUSEUM

Tubwell Row, Darlington DL1 1PD   (0325) 463795

Contact Alan Suddes, Assistant Curator

Admission Researchers by appointment

Hours Monday–Friday 10–1, 2–6; Thursday 10–1 only, Saturday 10–1, 2–5.30

Contents A few playbills and programmes relating to Darlington theatres, including the earliest known Darlington bill, dated 1768. Manuscript music notebooks of the late T. J. Hoggett of Leeds University.

DARLINGTON

54 DURHAM RECORD OFFICE. Darlington Branch

Darlington Branch Library, Crown Street, Darlington DL1 1ND

(0325) 462034 or 469858

Contact	Mrs J. Campbell, Assistant Archivist
Admission	Unrestricted. Advance booking required for evening or Saturday visit
Hours	Monday–Friday 9–1, 2.15–7; Saturday 9–1, 2.15–5
Contents	Da/Mu/2/39a Theatre Posters for Theatre Royal, Stockton (35) 1862–1875; Royal Albert Theatre, Middlesborough (8) 1868; Hartlepool Theatre (2) 1834; Town Hall, Kendal (1) 1860; New Theatre Whitby (1) 1831; Theatre Royal, North Shields (1) 1867; Tyne Theatre, Newcastle (1) 1881; Theatre Royal, Scarborouh (1) n.d.; Theatre Royal, Wolverhampton (1) 1866; Theatre Royal Durham (1) 1867; Theatre Royal, Darlington (1) 1938. D/DL/15/4 Notice advertising a play at the Theatre Royal, Wycliffe, Yorkshire, n.d.
Indexes	Place, subject and selected personal name indexes.
Catalogues	Interim or full lists arranged by record class and depositor.

DERBY

55 DERBY LOCAL STUDIES LIBRARY

25b Irongate, Derby DE1 3GL

(0332) 31111 Ext. 2184

Contact	Local Studies Librarian
Hours	Monday & Tuesday 9–7, Wednesday–Friday 9–5, Saturday 9.30–4
Contents	Collection of 18th and 19th century theatre bills (Parcel 216) Derby Grand Theatre — programmes and souvenirs 1896–1911, 6 volumes (8846–8851). Plays (Derby) Parcel 5x (Box 2). Assorted 20th century programmes and posters. Derby Playhouse Studio Company. *The Peartree Conspiracy* script, 1977 (BA 792). Bewley, Gordon and Hall, Irene Grand Opening, 1979. A radio documentary covering the history of Derby's Grand Theatre between March and November 1886 (BA 792). Lists of items in the private theatre collection of Harry Greatorex.
Indexes	General indexes include references to theatre material.

DONCASTER

56 DONCASTER ARCHIVES DEPARTMENT

King Edward Road, Doncaster DN4 0NA

(0302) 859811

Contact	Dr B. Barber, Archivist
Hours	Monday–Friday 9.30–12.30, 2–5
Contents	Legal and administrative records relating to the theatre in the Market Place, Doncaster built by the Corporation of Doncaster in

1776. Contents includes three letters from Tate Wilkinson, 1797–1799, concerning the payment of rent; draft leases 1867–1894, and specification for alterations, 1888, plus two handbills for 1786 and 1809. Floor plan of the Grand (formerly the Empire) Theatre, Doncaster 1898. Doncaster Area Theatre Trust Association. Report on a proposed theatre, 1969.

DONCASTER

57 DONCASTER CENTRAL LIBRARY

Waterdale, Doncaster DN1 3JE   (0302) 69123

Telex	54425
Contact	E. J. Chapman, Chief Librarian
Hours	Monday–Wednesday and Friday 9–8, Thursday 9–1, Saturday 9–5
Archives	Monday–Friday 9–5
Contents	Archives Department:

Archives Department:
5 plans of New Grand Theatre, 1898; Doncaster Theatre (1776–1900) built by the Corporation, references in the Corporation Minute Books from 1774, leases 1787–1873.
Reference Library:
Approximately 200 playbills relating to Doncaster Theatre, and 350 programmes relating to the Grand Theatre (1899–1959) and Arts Centre (1949 onwards).

DORCHESTER

58 DORCHESTER REFERENCE LIBRARY

Colliton Park, Dorchester, Dorset DT1 1XJ   (0305) 63131 Ext. 4448
After office hours (0305) 62734

Contact	Local Studies Librarian
Hours	Monday, Tuesday, Wednesday, Friday 9.30–7, Thursday 9.30–5, Saturday 9–1
Contents	Thomas Hardy Collection:

Thomas Hardy Collection:
Programmes of performances of dramatisations of Hardy's novels, 1882+ (approx. 50). Venues of performances — Dorchester, Weymouth, London, Cambridge and Salisbury.

Other ephemera in the collection includes:
posters, advertisements and publicity material associated with performances, also newspaper cuttings, reviews, correspondence and photographs of performances.

Local Ephemera Collection:
includes mainly modern material advertising performances by local amateur companies and professional touring companies,also programmes, press cuttings etc.

Dorchester Community Play material includes:

virtually all newspaper articles, reviews and letters from local and national papers, personal correspondence, publicity material associated with events leading to the productions (e.g. fund-raising events), programmes, posters, handouts, tickets, large collection of photographs.

Adams Collection:
Playbills for Theatre Royal, Weymouth 1797, 1804, 1859, 1867. Playbills for Theatre, Dorchester 1785, 1813. Scrapbook for Weymouth Theatre Royal.

Scrapbook for Dorset theatres:
these include letters, newspaper cuttings, photographs and photocopies of playbills, photographs of theatres, seating plans, and various information on dates of performances and performers etc. gathered by the compiler.

DORCHESTER
59 DORSET COUNTY RECORD OFFICE

County Hall, Dorchester   (0305) 3131 Ext. 4411

Contact	Hugh Jacques, County Archivist
Admission	Unrestricted. Appointments advisable.
Hours	Monday–Friday 9–1, 2–5
Contents	Indexes reveal references to drama in church, performed by strolling players etc; also text of a play performed by Dorchester schoolboys before the Bishop in 1623, and text of a mumming play as performed in Symondsbury in 1881. There are some references to players in the Quarter Sessions records and borough records. A few playbills.

DORCHESTER
60 DORSET NATURAL HISTORY AND ARCHAEOLOGICAL SOCIETY LIBRARY

Dorset County Museum, High West Street, Dorchester, Dorset   (0305) 62735

Contact	The Curator
Hours	Monday–Saturday 10–5
	Programmes and posters of performances in 19th century Dorset theatres. Programmes and some posters of performances of the novels of Thomas Hardy as plays, mostly (but by no means all) by the Hardy Players. Also manuscript and part books of some of the texts of these plays, with photographs and correspondence. The Thomas Hardy Memorial Collection also contains letters from such as G. B. Shaw, J. M. Barrie, Granville Barker, Robert Graves etc. concerning theatrical performances of Hardy material.
Indexes	Card index.

DUDLEY

61 DUDLEY PUBLIC LIBRARY, ARCHIVES AND LOCAL HISTORY DEPARTMENT

St. James's Road, Dudley, West Midlands DY1 1HL   (0384) 55433 Ext. 5526

Contact	Mrs Atkins, Mrs Matthews or Miss Williams
Hours	Monday, Wednesday, Friday 9–1, 2–5; Tuesday and Thursday 2–7; 1st and 3rd Saturdays in month 9.30–12.30 by appointment — materials must be ordered in advance.
Contents	Printed books and pamphlets (including theatre programmes): Miscellaneous programmes etc. relating to amateur productions, Programmes and posters relating to Dudley Opera House, Hippodrome Theatre, Midland Theatre Company, New Empire Palace, Empire Theatre and Dudley Little Theatre. Chris Gittins, *Theatres and cinemas in Stourbridge 1752–1952*, 1980. Posters relating to the Dudley Garrick Club. Miscellaneous Newscuttings Volumes. Register of Theatre Licences 1895–1947. Register of Theatrical Employers 1948–1975 (restricted access).
Indexes	Local Information Catalogue — index to articles in periodicals and Newscutting Books, arranged in alphabetical order of subject, Index to local newspapers 1870s–1890s.

DURHAM

62 DURHAM COUNTY RECORD OFFICE

County Hall, Durham DH1 5UL   (0385) 64411 Ext. 2474 or 2253

Contact	D. J. Butler, County Archivist
Availability	For consultation at times below
Hours	Monday, Tuesday, Thursday 8.45–4.45, Wednesday 8.45–8.30, Friday 8.45–4.15
Contents	D/He 54, Theatre programmes for the Royalty Theatre, London, 1896, and the Theatre Royal, Manchester 1895 (2 items). D/Lo/X61, Theatre programme for the Theatre Royal, Seaham Harbour, 1875 (1 item). D/X 189, Articles of Association of South Shields Theatre Company Ltd., 1865. D/NRC/Box 19, Deeds relating to conveyance of The Playhouse, Stockton, 1766 and 1787. Quarter Sessions Order Books have occasional entries relating to licences between 1751 and 1889.

EDINBURGH

63A EDINBURGH CITY LIBRARIES

Central Library, George IV Bridge, Edinburgh EH1 1EG   (031) 225 5584

Contact	A. Shearman, City Librarian
Hours	Monday–Friday 9–9, Saturday 9–1 (Central Home Reading Dept. Monday–Friday 9–8.30, Saturday 9–1)

| Contents | General library stock, plus approximately 2,600 playbills and 3,075 programmes and volumes of business records, histories, etc. The collection is strong on 18th and 19th century theatres, particularly the New Concert Hall, Canongate; Theatre Royal, Shakespeare Square and the Theatre Royal, Broughton Street. This material and other sources in the National Library of Scotland and the City Archives have, in effect, been indexed in the unpublished Library Association Fellowship thesis *The Edinburgh Stage, 1715–1820*' by Mrs Norma Armstrong. Modern theatre — Royal Lyceum, King's, Empire etc. are represented mainly by a wide press-cutting coverage; daybooks, playbills and programmes are also collected. Interesting collection of approximately 100 theatre postcards. |

EDINBURGH
63B   NATIONAL LIBRARY OF SCOTLAND
George IV Bridge, Edinburgh EH1 1EW   (031) 226 4531

Contact	The Superintendent of the Readers Services
Admission	By ticket. Temporary tickets are available
Hours	Monday–Friday 9.30–8.30, Saturday 9.30–1
Contents	National and copyright deposit library. Large collection of Edinburgh playbills, plus playbills for London and the provinces. Arranged by theatre.

ETON
64   ETON COLLEGE
Windsor SL4 6DB   (07535) 69991 Ext.38

Contact	Librarian
Admission	To graduate scholars only, by written appointment
Contents	Collection of pre-Restoration plays, all listed in *Greg.* MS catalogue compiled by Sir Robert Birley.

EXETER
65   DEVON RECORD OFFICE
Castle Street, Exeter EX4 3PQ   (0392) 53509

Contact	County Archivist
Admission	Unrestricted, but some items available at 24 hours notice only.
Hours	Monday–Thursday 9.30–5, Friday 9.30–4.30; 1st and 3rd Saturday of month (except those preceding bank holidays) 9.30–12
Contents	Programmes: Totnes Theatre, 2 for 1806 and 1821. Playbills: Theatre Royal, Plymouth, 1 for 1846. Prince's Theatre, Crediton, 1 for 1888. Share certificates' Barnstaple c.1835. Licences: Creditor for 1934 and 1948, Kingsteignton (amateur) 1886. Quarter Sessions records are partially indexed for 1803–1903. Depositions,

photographs, correspondence, newspaper cuttings: Exeter Theatre Fire 1887. Licences (some draft): Exeter, 1889–1905. Programmes: Exeter Theatre Royal, 1904–1941. Press Notices: Exeter Theatre Royal, c.1920–1930.

EXETER

66   EXETER CENTRAL LIBRARY

Central Library, Castle Street, Exeter   (0392) 53427

Contact	Jenny Broughton, Drama Librarian
Hours	Monday–Friday 9.30–8, Wednesday 9.30–6, Saturday 9.30–4
Contents	Northcott Theatre Collection; programmes and reviews for 1967 onwards. c.5,000 sets of plays (printed catalogue available). Spoken word cassette collection includes most plays commercially available, plus some Galsworthy and Arnold Bennett plays recorded by a local society.

EXETER

67   EXETER MUSIC AND DRAMA LIBRARY

Central Library, Castle Street, Exeter   (0392) 53427

Contact	Jenny Broughton, Drama Librarian
Hours	Monday–Friday 9.30–8, Wednesday 9.30–6, Saturday 9.30–4
Contents	The Music and Drama Library has programmes and reviews for the Northcott Theatre, Exeter, 1967+.

Theatre in Devon Collection:
an archive/information service on theatre (amateur and professional) in Devon, April 1974–1979, now in abeyance due to staff cuts. c.6,000 sets of plays.

The West Country Studies Library:
Playbills for Devon Theatre 1756–c.1890. 150 items.

Programmes for Devon theatre, amateur and professional c.1,900+, in main ephemera collections.

Indexes	Theatre in Devon Collection indexed by author, title and name of performing group. Handlist to West Country Studies collection in preparation.
Catalogues	Printed catalogue of playsets.

GATESHEAD

68   GATESHEAD CENTRAL LIBRARY

Prince Consort Road, Gateshead   (0632) 773478

Contact	Patrick Conway, Borough Librarian
Hours	Monday, Tuesday, Thursday, Friday 9.30–7.30, Wednesday 9.30–5, Saturday 9.30–1

| Contents | 160 playbills and programmes. |

GLASGOW

69 GLASGOW UNIVERSITY LIBRARY

Hillhead Street, Glasgow G12 8QE   (041) 339 8855 Ext. 6780

Contact	Dr Stephen Rawles
Admission	Researchers who are not members of the university are advised to make written application.
Hours	Term time: Monday–Friday 9–9.30, Saturday 9–12.30 Vacations: Monday–Friday 9–5, Saturday 9–12.30
Contents	Theatre materials in the general, open-access section of the library consist of:–

A working collection of c.4,000 volumes on the history and techniques of the performing arts (excluding music, opera and ballet, which are housed in the Music section); 100 serial titles of which 42 are current. Included are a fast growing film and television section, and works on the mass-media in general.

Dramatic texts and criticism of them, integrated into the various literature sections.

| Catalogues | Entries in the general library catalogues. |

GLASGOW

70 GLASGOW UNIVERSITY LIBRARY. Special Collections Department

Hillhead Street, Glasgow G12 8QE   (041) 339 8855 Ext. 5630

Contact	P. Escreet
Admission	To outside scholars and members of the theatre profession on written application. Available for consultation and photocopying where feasible within copyright regulations.
Hours	Term time: Monday–Friday 9.15–9.15, Saturday 9.15–12.15 Vacations: Monday–Friday 9.15–4.45, Saturday 9.15–12.15
Contents	The Special Collections Department houses the Scottish Theatre Archive, plus a considerable amount of theatre material scattered through other collections:

Theatre material in the Special Collections:
Farmer Collection includes photographs, programmes, playbills and other items.
Ephemera Collection — mainly playbills and programmes.

Manuscripts include:–
Barrie, J. M. *The Flight of Mr Lapraik, The Little Minister, A Well Remembered Voice.* Boswell, the younger, James. *The Grinners, The Seige of Carthage.* Nichols, J. *Death of Themistocles.* Waddie, Charles. *Dunbar, the King's Advocate.* Letters of James Bridie, Joanna Baillie. Papers of Margaret Morris,

Joan Ure.
Periodicals — Some 19th century titles.
Catalogues: General catalogues, Manuscript Catalogue, Ephemera Catalogue.

Scottish Theatre Archive:

Contact: Miss E. M. Watson   Ext. 6758
Contents: Playtexts — published, stage manuscripts, typescripts, prompt copies (c.1,000) including James Bridie's *The Anatomist*.
Programme Collection (including daybills) — mostly 20th century. c.2,000.
Papers etc. belonging to Prof. James F. Arnott, Robin Millar, G. Bottomley, Robert Bain, Molly Urquhart.
Theatre companies:- The contents varies according to the company but may include general administrative papers, play scripts including prompt copies, programmes, press-cuttings, photographs, and production material. The companies are: Citizens' Theatre Company, Royal Lyceum Company, Glasgow Jewish Institute Players, Glasgow Unit, Scottish National Players, Curtain Theatre, Park Theatre, 7:84 (Scotland), Wildcat. Material related to Scottish Community Drama Association and other amateur groups.
Printed Books — These cover theatre in Britain. c.200
Periodicals — Some 20th century periodicals, not always complete runs.

Catalogues   General catalogues, a Play Text catalogue is being compiled.

Note: A Directory of Scottish Theatre Collections has been prepared for publication.

GLASGOW

71 MITCHELL LIBRARY. Glasgow Room

North Street, Glasgow G3 7DN   (041) 248 7030

Contact   R. Gillespie, Assistant Director Reference Services

Availability   On request at times below

Hours   Monday–Friday 9.30–9, Saturday 9.30–5

Contents   Printed texts of 86 pantomimes, c.16,000 programmes and playbills.

Guides   *Glasgow Theatres and Music Halls: a guide*. 1980. Alphabetical listing by theatre name giving building details, dates, management, sources of information. (Typescript)

GLASGOW

72 PEOPLE'S PALACE MUSEUM

Glasgow Green, Glasgow G40 1AT (041) 554 0223

Contact Elspeth King, Deputy Keeper of Local History

Availability Loan facilities to individual organisations, subject to certain conditions.

Hours Monday–Saturday 10–5, Sundays 2–5

Contents Miscellaneous collection relating to Scottish music hall and vaudeville including:

The Dow Collection of Theatre programmes. 948 programmes for theatre and pantomime, 1904–1935, mainly Glasgow.

Programmes relating to the following Glasgow theatres: The Glasgow Hippodrome; Glasgow Empire Palace; Her Majesty's Theatre, Main Street; Prince of Wales Theatre; The Folly, Dunlop Street; Hengler's Circus; The Royal Princess, 1882–1895; The Scotia Music Hall and Variety Theatre 1889–1895; The Gaiety, 1882–1895; The Theatre Royal, 1812–1936; The Citizens; The Grand Theatre, Cowcaddens; The King's Theatre, 1925–1962; The Royalty Theatre, 1883–1894; The Metropole Theatre; Jimmy Logan's Metropole; The New Star Theatre of Varieties and People's Palace.

The Frutin Collection of posters and programmes c.1930–1960s, gifted by Alec Frutin, Manager of the late Metropole, Stockwell Street.

A small collection of posters and programmes relates to the swinger of Indian clubs, David Shields, 1899–1914.

Substantial collection of posters and large bills, relating to the Royal Princess, 1890–1935.

Fittings from the Palace Theatre, Gorbals (designed by Bertie Crewe c.1904) including the cash desk, poster-boxes, lights, finger plates, mosaic from proscenium arch and part of the roof canvas (latter item under restoration).

Collection of material relating to Billy Connolly.

Miscellaneous photographs, drawings and paintings.

A small collection relating to the cinema in Glasgow, 1910–1940.

GLASOW

73 ROYAL SCOTTISH ACADEMY OF MUSIC AND DRAMA. Library

St. George's Place, Glasgow G2 1BS (051) 332 4101 Ext. 37

Contact Drama Librarian, Marian J. Fordon

Admission Available to anyone for reference use.

Hours Term time: Monday, Wednesday, Friday 9.30–5.30, Tuesday, Thursday 9.30–7.30. Vacations: Monday-Friday 9.30–4.30

Contents	Approximately 2,920 volumes of plays, 4,500 books about drama (acting, costume, makeup, production and technical, pictorial social history, television, radio, film, history of theatre, drama in education, poetry, criticism, biography), approximately 100 audio-visual items (including spoken word recordings) approximately 25 periodicals.

Approximately 25 programmes covering Glasgow theatres from Dec. 1881–Oct. 1901 and approximately 80 programmes covering performances by the Scottish National Players and various items about them, for the period 1921–1940.

The School of Drama itself holds programmes of student performances from 1950 (when the school started). The bulk of other archival material is held in the University of Strathclyde and consists of three types:
1. Minute books of the Academy Board including discussion of the Athenaeum Theatre and building.
2. Programmes of performances in the Athenaeum Theatre from 1893–1950s.
3. Cuttings books covering the period 1893–c.1947.

Unfortunately some of the volumes from each of these types of material are missing, so no sequence is complete.

GLOUCESTER
74   GLOUCESTER LIBRARY
Brunswick Road, Gloucster GL1 1HT   (0452) 426977

Contact	Reference Librarian
Hours	Monday, Tuesday, Thursday 9–8, Wednesday & Friday 9–5, Saturday 9–1
Contents	Miscellaneous material scattered through County Local History Collections.
Catalogues	Austin, Roland. *Gloucestershire Collection Catalogue,* 1928 plus two later manuscript catalogues.

GLOUCESTER
75   GLOUCESTERSHIRE RECORD OFFICE
Worcester Street, Gloucester   (0452) 21444 Ext. 229

Contact	Dr J. H. S. Smith, County Archivist
Hours	Monday–Friday 9–5 (open until 8 pm on Thursdays)
Contents	MSS scripts (2), Playbills and programmes (7), Licensing records (6), Business records (6), Letters (3). D2025 Watson Theatre Co. (Gloucester, Cheltenham etc.) 4 boxes. D4655 Archives of Gloucester Operatic and Dramatic Society 1913–83. D4856 Detailed records of Gloucestershire amateur dramatic societies activities.

GRIMSBY

76A GRIMSBY CENTRAL REFERENCE LIBRARY

Town Hall Square, Grimsby DN31 1HG (0472) 40405

Contact	D. Wattam
Hours	Monday–Friday 10–8, Saturday 9–4
Contents	Miscellaneous items relating the Caxton Players; Empire Theatre, Cleethorpes; Palace Theatre, Grimsby; Prince of Wales Theatre, Grimsby; Theatre Royal, Grimsby; Tivoli Theatre, Grimsby. *Records of plays and players in Lincolnshire 1300–1585,* edited by Stanley J. Kahrl. (Collections of the Malone Society Vol. VIII) 1974.

GUILDFORD

76B NATIONAL RESOURCE CENTRE FOR DANCE

University of Surrey, Guildford GU2 5XH (0483) 571281

Contact	Research Officer for further information.
Admission	By appointment
Contents	The Centre is in the process of establishing the major resource on all aspects of dance, and has a wide range of books, periodicals, programmes, press-cuttings etc. Records of dance holdings in other libraries are being collected.

HARROGATE

77 NORTH YORKSHIRE COUNTY REFERENCE LIBRARY

Divisional Headquarters, Victoria Avenue, Harrogate, N. Yorks.(0423) 502744

Contact	Divisonal Organiser Reference
Hours	Monday–Friday 9–7, Thursday 9–5, Saturday 9–1
Contents	Playbills (original and photocopies) for Georgian Theatre. Grand Opera House (now Harrogate Theatre) programmes 1900+, also cuttings etc. Royal Hall bills and programmes for mostly 1920s and 30s.
Indexes	Index to local newspapers 1970+.

HARTLEPOOL

78 GRAY ART GALLERY AND MUSEUM

Clarence Road, Hartlepool, Cleveland TS24 8BT (0429) 266522 Ext. 259

Contact	The Curator
Admission	By written application
Hours	Wednesday 9–12 noon
Contents	Box 150 Theatre Royal and the Gaiety Theatre, West Hartlepool.

Box 151   Empress Theatre of Varieties, Hartlepool, Hippodrome Theatre, Stockton, Theatrical and variety agents.

Box 152   Other theatres in towns in the North East, posters which do not indicate name of theatre, posters of performances which took places in saloons, inns etc. material relating to Billy Purvis, the Geordie Clown, cards for benefit nights and artistes.

Box 153   Amateur dramatics

Box 154   Amateur operatics

Boxes 155–158 Concerts, concert parties etc.

Box 159   Assemblies, balls, cinemas, dioramas etc.

Much of the material came from the collection of Robert Wood, a local historian. Theatre material in the John George Joicey Museum in Newcastle also came from this collection, which came originally from a printer's workshop in Hartlepool, much of it the work of John Procter c.1830–1890.

Indexes   Card index with a card for each item of ephemera. Each box includes a handlist of its contents, grouped into subject headings. These handlists can be copied and sent to researchers.

HAVERFORDWEST

79   PEMBROKESHIRE RECORD OFFICE

The Castle, Haverfordwest, Dyfed   (0437) 3707

Contact   John Owen, Assistant Archivist

Hours   Monday–Thursday 9–4.45, Friday 9–4.15, 1st and 3rd Saturday in each month 9.30–12.30

Contents   Approximately 12 MSS of plays by Florence Howell (D/HOW); 27 letters and newscuttings and 2 programmes relating to her plays.

HAWARDEN

80   CLWYD RECORD OFFICE

The Old Rectory, Hawarden, Deeside, Clwyd   (0244) 532364

Contact   A. G. Veysey, County Archivist

Hours   Monday–Thursday 9–4.45, Friday 9–4.15

Contents   D/E/1542/217 Wynnstay Theatre, Ruabon — broadsheet 1778. D/CL/100 New Theatre, Holywell — playbill 1789 (photocopy). NT/755 photo of poster advertising theatre at Red Lion Inn, St. Asaph, 1806. D/E/1542/382 Performance of Cinderella at Acton Park, Wrexham — playbill, 1859. D/DM/405/1 Programme for performance of Rhys Lewis (written by Daniel Owen) at Trefriw, Denbs. 1886. D/LR/9 Prestatyn Curtain Players — programmes, photos, etc. 1939–49. D/E/(addn1) papers of Philip Yorke re his theatrical productions, 1930s. D/DG Buckley Amateur Pantomime Company — manuscript scripts (also programmes, playbills) 1932–59. Papers of Dennis Griffiths on amateur drama in North Wales. Tapes and photographs of Buckley Amateur Pantomime Co. CC/TC/ Theatre Clwyd posters, programmes, etc. for 1976–82.

HERTFORD

81 HERTFORDSHIRE RECORD OFFICE

Room 204, County Hall, Hertford SG13 8DE   (0992) 54242 Ext. 413

Contact   Peter Walne, County Archivist

Hours   Monday–Thursday 9.15–5.15, Friday 9.15–4.30

Contents   Include Minutes of Playhouses Ltd., Welwyn, 1927–8 and 1933–6 (Ref. D/EFf B63–4). A few playbills of various dates, mainly relating to local performances not held in theatres. Programme and photographs of the cast of the Royal Command Performance of *Money* by Lord Lytton, played before the Kaiser, 1910, (D/EK W15). Typescript and manuscript copies of *Junius, or the Household Gods* for presentation at the Prince's Theatre, 1885 (D/EK W42). Autograph manuscripts of other Lytton plays, some unpublished.

HORNCHURCH

82 HORNCHURCH BRANCH LIBRARY

44 North Street, Hornchurch, Essex RM11 1TD   (04024) 52248

Contact   Librarian

Hours   Monday, Tuesday, Thursday, Friday 9.30–8, Saturday 9.30–5

Contents   Queen's Theatre, Hornchurch, Archive:
             A major archive of the productions of this theatre which opened in 1953. As far as possible the archive has been arranged in 'Production Packages', each pack containing all the available information on each play. The Archive contains over 500 theatre programmes, approximately 4,000 photographs, posters, print blocks, slides, scripts, set design models, scrapbooks, newscuttings etc. The Archive covers 1953 to date and is ongoing.

Indexes   To date some 20,000 catalogue cards have been produced covering plays, names of artists, production staff etc. The Categories Index ranges from Acting Stage Managers to Youth Drama Instructors.

HUDDERSFIELD

83A TOLSON MEMORIAL MUSEUM

Ravensknowle Park, Huddersfield   (0484) 530591

Contact   Stephen Caunce

| Hours | Monday-Saturday 10–5, Sunday 1–5 |
| Contents | 28 theatre bills between 1803–1961 (but mainly mid–19th century) relating to local theatres and a Halifax theatre. Some photographs of exteriors, one interior. |

HUDDERSFIELD
83B   WEST YORKSHIRE ARCHIVES
Kirklees District Central Library, Princess Alexandra Walk, Huddersfield
HD1 2SU   (0484) 513808 Ext. 207

Contact	Miss J. Burhouse
Hours	Monday–Thursday 9–8, Friday 9–4. Saturday by prior arrangements only
Contents	Dewsbury Theatre Royal B/DTR: Theatre bills c.1869–1871 (7 items). Wages book 1928–1932. Huddersfield Theatre Royal: Minutes 1926–1929, Balance Sheets 1903–1933 (by production), Profit and loss file 1918–1935, Cash books 1920–1932, Ledgers 1924–1933, Memoranda 1930–1936 (re. advertising) Additional KC64. Album 1923–4 (commendations by visiting performers).

HULL *see* KINGSTON UPON HULL

HUNTINGDON
84   HUNTINGDON COUNTY RECORD OFFICE
Grammar School Walk, Huntingdon PE18 6LF   (0480) 52181 Ext. 4842
                                                        (0480) 51975 (direct line)

Contact	A. Hill, Senior Archivist
Hours	Monday–Friday 9–5. Saturday (by appointment only) 9–1
Contents	Insurance policy for £550 for the building of a theatre in Huntingdon, 1829, 24/20/25. Abstract of Title of Mrs Fanny Maria Robertson to the theatre in Huntingdon, 1845, 24/20/17. Agreement for sale of the theatre and a few other papers relating to this, 1845, 24/20/21 and following. Title to Lady O. B. Sparrow to the grounds on which the theatre stood at Huntingdon 1851, DDM/21B/9 and a document re. rights of way there, 1852, DDM67/4. Petitions of Thomas Shaftoe Robertson, Manager of the Huntingdon, Lincoln etc. Co. of Comedians, to perform in Huntingdon. 1820, 1822 & 1827, H'don Borough 12/7, 20/17. Glass plates of: Miss Duncan's Theatre Group (1), Brampton Park Theatre Group (8), Lloyds School Theatre Group, St. Ives (1), late 19th & early 20th centuries, Whitney collection. Interior & stage of the Little Gem Theatre, Huntingdon (1). Scouts: Boys' Theatricals

(1), c.1909. Somersham Mystery Play, 1977. Petition of Fanny Maria Robertson, actress for a licence for her company to perform in Huntingdon Theatre, 1836, O/S Papers 1836. Posters of: *The Busy Body*, played by Mr Richardson's Co of Comedians at the George Hotel, Huntingdon, 1781, 518/. *Tekeli & The World* at the Huntingdon Theatre, 1808, Posters. The Moor Theatre, St. Neots. 1896, 143/. Verse by Richard Brinsley Sheridan. 1811, DDM17/1/3. 6 cartoons of John Liston, the actor, c.1825, DDM17/2. Shakespeare: proposed memorial — letters and papers (some in German) including An Ode for his Three Hundredth Birthday. 1864, DDM/10B/31. Diaries of the second wife of 10th Marquis of Huntley, which contains a few comments on plays she saw in London. 1893. Miscellaneous modern programmes.

KINGSTON UPON HULL

85   UNIVERSITY OF HULL. Brynmor Jones Library

Cottingham Road, Hull HU6 7RX   (0482) 46311

Admission   Temporary ticket available to non-members on application

Hours   Term time: Monday–Friday 9–9.45
             Vacations: Monday–Friday 9–5.30

Contents   includes historical collection of ephemera relating to Hull and Yorkshire theatres in the 19th and early 20th centuries.

KINGSTON UPON HULL

86   UNIVERSITY OF HULL. Drama Department

Cottingham Road, Hull, Northumberland HU6 7RX   (0482) 497615

Contact   Donald Roy

Admission   In term time only to scholars and bona fide research students

Hours   9.30–5

Contents   Production archive relating to all departmental stage productions, and to performances in the Department's theatre by visiting professional companies and solo artists.

KINGSTON UPON HULL

87   WILBERFORCE HOUSE

25 High Street, Kingston upon Hull   (0482) 222737

Contact   I. Rutherford, Keeper of Social History

Hours   Monday–Saturday 10–5, Sunday 1.30–4.30

Contents   Theatre bills for Theatre Royal, Hull, 1764–c.1890. Theatre bills for minor Hull theatres, especially 1800–50. Sketchbook of scenery from Theatre Royal, Hull 1816. Miscellaneous collection of programmes and handbills. Theatre bills from Beverley, Patrington, Bridlington and Burton Constable, as well as amateur dramatics elsewhere in the East Riding.

Indexes   A5 card index. Handlists of collection available.

KINGSTON-UPON-THAMES
88 KINGSTON-UPON-THAMES HERITAGE CENTRE
Fairfield West, Kingston-upon-Thames, Surrey   (01) 546 5386

Contact   Marion Shipley, Curator

Hours   Monday–Saturday 10–5

Contents   Press cuttings and complete set of playbills on the Royal County Theatre, cuttings and playbills for Kingston Empire. Typescript history of the Royal County Theatre. Ten items on local pageants and pantomimes. Some press cuttings on Overground Theatre.

Card Index   To references in the *Surrey Comet*.

KINGSTON-UPON-THAMES
89 SURREY RECORD OFFICE
County Hall, Penrhyn Road, Kingston-upon-Thames, Surrey KT1 2DN
                                                  (01) 546 1050 Ext. 3561

Contact   Dr D. B. Robinson, County Archivist, The Search Room

Admission   Free

Hours   Monday, Wednesday and Friday 9.30–4.45, closed on Thursdays, Saturday (2nd and 4th in month) 9.30–12.30, by appointment only.

Contents   Information on the licensing of places of entertainment in Surrey in the Quarter Session records.

Catalogue   In the Search Room.

LANCASTER
90 LANCASTER LOCAL HISTORY COLLECTION
District Library Headquarters, Market Square, Lancaster LA1 1HY
                                                  (0524) 63266/7

Contact   Miss U. B. Murphy, District Librarian

Hours   Monday, Thursday & Friday 9.30–7, Tuesday 9.30–5, Wednesday and Saturday 9.30–4

Contents   Lancaster Theatre bills:
                 1772, 2 not dated but c.1773, 1775 (7), 1788, 1790, 1794, 1797 (4), 1800, 1801, 1809, 1822 (3), 1823, 1826, 1830, 1832, 1833. Bill for the Olympic Circus, Lancaster, 1st April 1822. Bill for variety at the Hippodrome, Lancaster, 17th April 1911. Cartmel Theatre Bills — 1 dated 18th July 1811, the other not dated but probably earlier. Poem to be recited by Mr Nunden at his benefit on 17th August 1785 at the Theatre, Lancaster,

called *John Gilpin of Cheapside going farther than he intended: a droll story* (Broadsheet). Lancaster Sept. Meeting: a new song sung by Mr Bailey at the Theatre Royal Lancaster (Broadsheet c.1800). *Royalty Theatre, Morecambe: Twenty five years of repertory,* Lancaster, Barber, 1950, 31p. — this consists mainly of *The Royalty and the Players,* by George Laughton, which is a short history of the theatre from 1898–1950.

LANCASTER
91 MEDIEVAL ENGLISH THEATRE COLLECTION
Housed at Department of English Language and Medieval Literature, University of Lancaster, Bailrigg, Lancs.   (0524) 65201 Ext. 314

Contact	Mrs M. A. Twycross
Admission	On application
Hours	Monday–Friday 10–5
Contents	The E. Martin Browne Collection:

Scrapbooks, producers' notebooks and texts, slides, tapes and other material belonging to the late E. Martin Browne, and relating to his productions of medieval religious drama, especially of the original productions of the York Cycle from 1951 onwards.

Medieval English Theatre Archive:

Programmes, posters and some production material relating to other productions of medieval drama in Britain and elsewhere from c.1970 onwards.

LANCASTER
92 UNIVERSITY OF LANCASTER. University Library
Bailrigg, Lancaster LA1 4YH   (0524) 65201

Contact	Ms L. M. Newman
Admission	On request to the Librarian
Hours	Term time: Monday, Tuesday, Thursday & Friday 8.45–10, Wednesday 9.30–10, Sunday 2–7
	Vacations: Monday, Tuesday, Thursday 9–5.15, Wednesday 9.30–5.15, Friday 9–4.30
Contents	Material corresponds to teaching and research requirements within the university and its Department of Theatre Studies. The University Library holds no archives.

LEEDS
93 ABBEY HOUSE MUSEUM
Kirkstall, Leeds 5   (0532) 755821

Contact	Mrs June E. Bridgwater

Hours	Summer: Monday–Saturday 10–6, Sunday 2–5
	Winter: Monday–Saturday 10–5, Sunday 2–5
Content	19th and 20th century play and concert bills relating to Leeds; also some miscellaneous bills.
Note	Collection uncatalogued.

LEEDS

94 LEEDS CENTRAL LIBRARY

Municipal Buildings, Leeds LS1 3AB   (0532) 462016 (Reference Library)

Contact	Reference Library
Hours	Monday–Wednesday 9–9, Thursday–Friday 9–5.30, Saturday 9–4
Contents	5,500 playbills and an unnumbered collection of programmes from Leeds theatres. (Incomplete indexes to performance, dramatists, and actors.) MSS lecture notes and a MSS history of Leeds theatres by Alf Mattison.

LEEDS

95 UNIVERSITY OF LEEDS. University Library

Leeds, West Yorkshire LS2 9JT   (0532) 431751

Contact	The Librarian
Admission	On written application
Hours	Monday–Friday 9–5
Contents	**Brotherton Collection:**

There is a great quantity of potentially relevant material here: the following is a selection of some important groups: (i) Printed plays c.1600–1750: a very comprehensive collection of first and early editions, some with contemporary annotation, e.g. James Shirley *Loves cruelite,* 1640; prompt copy. Sir William Killigrew *Four new playes,* 1666; with major autograph alterations by the author for a projected new edition. (ii) Autograph MSS of theatrical and other writings by Theodosius and Frederick Forrest, mid to late 18th century. (iii) Collection of Leeds theatre bills, 1804–46. (iv) Letters of James Sheridan Knowles to James Muspratt, 1831–62. (v) Pierce Egan the younger *The blind lover;* autograph MS. (vi) Collection of letters to Bram Stoker and Sir Henry Irving, largely in connection with the Lyceum Theatre. (vii) Collection of letters to Henry Arthur Jones. (viii) Lady Gregory *The golden apple;* autograph MS. (ix) Dramatic papers of John Mackendrick.

Special Collections:
(i) Collection of playbills, mainly relating to London, 1806–1871. 75 items. Handlist available. (ii) 16 bound volumes of programmes principally for concerts, opera and ballet, mainly

in London, c.1930–c.1960. (iii) Collection of programmes, some only as cuttings, mainly of provincial concerts and opera, 1876–1936. 262 items. Handlist available. (iv) Programmes of the Glyndebourne Festival opera, 1952–1981.

Videotapes:
(i) Collections of extracts and complete plays prepared for M.A. Drama courses. (ii) G. Wilson Knight: commentaries on and extracts from Shakespeare's tragedies, acted by himself. (iii) Discussion between Wilson Knight and Derek Valentine.

LEICESTER

96 LEICESTER POLYTECHNIC. Scraptoft Site Library

Scraptoft Campus, Scraptoft, Leicester LE7 9SU   (0533) 431011 Ext. 300

Contact	Jane Brittain
Admission	Reference use. Applications to librarian for borrowing facilities.
Hours	Term time: Monday 8.45–7, Tuesday–Thursday 8.45–9, Friday 8.45–5. Vacations: Monday–Friday 9–5
Contents	Approximately 21,000 books, plus cassettes, videos and periodicals in broad subject areas of music, drama, dance and arts administration.

LEICESTER

97 LEICESTERSHIRE COLLECTION

Information Centre, Bishop Street, Leicester LE1 6AA   (0533) 556699

Contact	A. W. Stevenson Leicestershire Studies Librarian
Hours	Monday–Friday 9–7, Saturday 9–4
Contents	Approximately 200 programmes and 130 playbills of Leicester theatres. General library stock.

LEICESTER

98 LEICESTERSHIRE RECORD OFFICE

57 New Walk, Leicester LE1 7JB   (0533) 554566

Admission	Material available on one week's notice.
Hours	Monday–Thursday 9.15–5, Friday 9.15–4.45, Saturday 9.15–12.15
Contents	Approximately 150 programmes and playbills. Opera score *The Crescent and the Cross*. Records of the Theatre Royal, Leicester: 12 items including minute books. Records of Emma Theatre Company 1971–81.

LEIGH

99 WIGAN RECORD OFFICE

Town Hall, Leigh, Lancashire WN7 2DY   Leigh 672421 Ext. 266

Contact	A. Gillies
Hours	Monday–Friday 10–4
Contents	A few programmes, newspaper cuttings and photographs of theatres and music halls in the Wigan and Leigh areas.

LEWES

100 EAST SUSSEX COUNTY RECORD OFFICE

The Maltings, Castle Precincts, Lewes BN7 1YT (Lewes) 475400 Ext. 12/369

Contact	C. R. Davey, County Records Officer
Admission	Unrestricted
Hours	Monday–Thursday 8.45–4.45, Friday 8.45–4.15
Contents	1. Eastbourne Pier Co. Ltd., company records, 1865–1976
	2. Brighton Theatre Royal, programmes, 1906–1981 (incomplete)
	3. Lewes Little Theatre Ltd., Records, 1938–1981
	4. 18th & 19th century Quarter Sessions rolls and order books, containing licences for theatres in East Sussex
	5. Town directories; 19th & 20th century newspaper files
	6. Passing references in a wide range of sources, e.g. family letters, diaries and deeds, and town records.

LINCOLN

101 LINCOLN LOCAL STUDIES COLLECTION

Reference Library, Free School Lane, Lincoln LN2 1EZ

(0522) 33541 Ext. 38

Contact	Miss S. Gates
Hours	Monday, Tuesday, Thursday, Friday 9–7 Wednesday 9–1, Saturday 9–12.30
Contents	c.540 playbills for Lincolnshire theatres ranging in date from c.1754 to 1913. Chronological index, author and title index on cards.

LINCOLN

102 LINCOLNSHIRE ARCHIVES OFFICE

The Castle, Lincoln   (0522) 25158

Contact	Dr G. A. Knight, Principal Archivist
Availability	Free access subject to usual acknowledgements in publications
Hours	Monday–Friday 9.30–4.45
Contents	Includes playbills and programmes. Spalding playbills 1778–96

(misc Don. 94). Smedley family: accounts, correspondence, playbills etc. at Sleaford and on tour in Lincolnshire and neighbouring counties in the first half of the 19th century (LLHS 38). Licensing records among the records of the local authorities of the area.

LINCOLN

103 MUSEUM OF LINCOLNSHIRE LIFE

The Old Barracks, Burton Road, Lincoln LN1 3LY   (0522) 28448

Contact   P. R. Cousins, Keeper of Social History

Hours   Monday–Saturday 10–5.30, Sunday 2–5.30

Contents   Miscellaneous items including 4 playbills for local theatres. A number of programmes for London theatres (1930s–1950s) including suburban theatres at Streatham, Penge and Lewisham.

Indexes   Included in museum catalogue.

LIVERPOOL

104 LIVERPOOL PUBLIC LIBRARY

William Brown Street, Liverpool L3   (051) 207 2147/3163/0036

Hours   Monday–Friday 9–9, Saturday 9–5

Liverpool Public Library is one of the major libraries in the country, its stock is divided between a number of specialist departments and theatre material may be found in three of these:–

(a) Art Library
     includes general published works on the theatre arts.

(b) International Library
     contains the Drama Collection of play sets and single copies of plays, and literary criticism.

(c) Record Office
     see below.

LIVERPOOL PUBLIC LIBRARY. Record Office

Address, telephone number and hours as above.

Contact   Miss Janet Smith, Archivist

Contents   Theatre material is scattered according to format and collection, it includes: Programmes, playbills, posters, photographs, illustrations, paintings, written material and some archive material for the numerous theatres that have existed in the city since the 18th century.

Indexes   Internal catalogues.

LONDON

105A ARTS COUNCIL OF GREAT BRITAIN. Information and Research Library

105 Picadilly, London W1V 0AU   (01) 629 9495

Contact	Head of Information and Research: Gillian Dave Information Officer: Rod Fisher, Librarian: Barbara Costanzo
Admission	By prior appointment
Hours	Monday–Friday 10–5
Contents	The Library's specialist collection has been developed in support of the work and objects of the Arts Council and its staff, and is related principally to cultural policy, arts administration, and social and economic aspects of the arts, both in Britain and overseas. The collection comprises:

(a) **Books, Reports and Papers.** Over 10,000 books, reports and papers, dissertations and offprints on the arts.

(b) **Periodicals.** The Library receives over 200 periodicals, including Regional Arts Associations' newspapers and magazines, through subscription or donation. These are scanned and items of interest referred to in a current awareness journal, *Arts Documentation Monthly*.

(c) **Other Documentation.** (i) Arts Centres — Files containing information such as the history, building plans, programmes publications for over 200 arts centres in England, Wales and Scotland. (ii) Overseas Cultural Policy — Files containing documentation on the arts policy, work and expenditure of foreign nations. The collection is strongest in material from the U.S.A. (iii) Council of Europe — A substantial collection of approximately 300 reports and papers on cultural policy, expenditure and decentralisation, animation, creativity and communication issued by the Council of Europe. (iv) Surveys — Approximately 175 audience and other surveys, primarily theatre-based. (v) Legislation — Copies of Acts of Parliament, Green and White Papers and Government reports related to the arts. (vi) Lectures, Speeches and Papers — A collection of offprints, etc. of speeches and articles both about the Council and the arts generally.

(d) **Registers.** The Information section maintains indexes or registers in various fields e.g. on-going research, arts administration training courses, disability organisations and projects.

(e) **Publications.** A regular *Information Bulletin* is issued with the intention of keeping those working in the arts informed of Arts Council policy and work, developments at the RAAs and overseas, new publications and documentation, research projects, conferences and courses. *Arts Documentation Monthly* was introduced in 1976 to provide a regular selected listing of arts articles abstracted from periodicals received by the Information and Research Reference Library. *Reference Sheets* are compiled periodically, which list sources of information on specific arts subjects or provide select bibliographies on such areas as theatre, community arts, fund-raising, sponsorship, marketing and cultural policy. The section also issues directories such as the *Directory of Arts Centres* and *Directory of Arts Projects* on an annual basis. Other regular publications include the *Set Plays and Books List* and the *Guide to Awards and Schemes.* The Council's research staff issue regular statistics on attendances at subsidised theatre, opera and dance, and produce an annual *playlist* giving details of productions, numbers of performances and popularity. The section also issues occasional *Statistical Reports* and *Research Reports.* Lists of these can be obtained from the Information Office at the Arts Council. In addition, the Council has periodically published reports on various aspects of theatre, and a list of these and its other publications can be obtained from the Publications Section at the Arts Council.

LONDON

105B   BARNET PUBLIC LIBRARIES. Local History Collection

Hendon Library, The Burroughs, Hendon, London NW4 4BE

(01) 202 5625 Ext. 55

Contact	The Archivist
Hours	By appointment
Contents	Plans, programmes and photographs of the Golders Green Theatre. Photographs of the Orpheaum Theatre, Golders Green.

LONDON

105C   THE BEAR GARDENS MUSEUM OF THE SHAKESPEAREAN STAGE

Bear Gardens, Bankside, London SE1 9EB   (01) 928 6342

Contact	Museum Manager
Admission	£1 (50p OAPs, students, children and unwaged)
Hours	Tuesday–Saturday 10–5.30, Sunday 2–6
Contents	The Museum's permanent exhibition focuses on the history of the Elizabethan and Jacobean stage. Models and contemporary visual

material tell the story of the playhouses, players and audiences from 1576 to 1642.

LONDON
106   BRITISH ARCHITECTURAL LIBRARY
Royal Institute of British Architects, 66 Portland Place, London W1N 4AD
(01) 580 5533

Admission   To members, and to the public as a reference library.

Hours   Monday 10–5, Tuesday, Thursday 10–8, Friday 10–7, Saturday 10–1.30

Contents   Includes approx. 1,000 monographs on the architecture of theatres, cinemas, concert halls etc. and stage design; approx. 800 current architectural and design journals.

Journal titles specially on theatre architecture are:
Buhnentechnische Rundschau 1961–
Cue 1979–
Scena nos. 31–34
Tabs 1959–
Theatre design and technology 1959–
Theatre notebook 1945–

The library's photograph collection contains many photographs of theatre and cinema buildings.

Indexes   Card catalogues of books, and to periodical articals 1934–.

Publications   The library publishes a quarterly index to periodical articles, cumulating annually, entitled *Architectural Periodicals Index*. This index is also available for internal computer searching, and will be available on a commercial data-base from 1986.

see also
ROYAL INSTITUTE OF BRITISH ARCHITECTS. Drawings Collection

LONDON
107   BRITISH BROADCASTING CORPORATION REFERENCE LIBRARY. (Drama Section)
Room C135, Woodlands, 80 Wood Lane, London W12 0TT   (01) 743 8080

Contact   BBC Data Sales

Admission   To BBC Staff; the library is not open to the public. Outside researchers wishing to obtain admission should make written application to BBC Data Sales at the above address.

Contents   Approximately 10,000 printed play texts, plus histories and biographies; an extensive collection of programmes for the 19th and 20th centuries. Files of 30 theatre journals.

Catalogues   Card catalogue. Card index to periodical articles which includes reviews and illustrations.

LONDON

108 BRITISH BROADCASTING CORPORATION. Hulton Picture Library

35 Marylebone High Street, London W1M 4AA   (01) 927 4735

Contact	The Librarian, J. D. Lee
Hours	Monday to Friday 9.30–5.30
Contents	This huge general collection (over 9 million pictures) includes many engravings and photographs of theatrical subjects. Strongest on personalities but some scenes often in rehearsal. Coverage from early times to 1981, but stronger on the earlier periods than on the later, which depends on newspaper coverage by *Evening Standard* which is one of the collections held.

Specialist theatre material includes:–
photographs by Baron, Gordon Anthony (c.1935–55), Dennis de Marney (c.1940–58), Sasha (1924–40).

The general collections, London Stereoscopic Co., Topical Press, and Picture Post, all had photographers who took theatre and related topics — music hall, pantomime, puppets etc.

Arrangement is by Gibbs-Smith classification, basically alphabetico-classed, under THEATRE. All collections amalgamated in print form, separate as negatives. The arrangement is self-indexing, specialised indexes being prepared as required.

Publications	Descriptive brochure.
Note	*Theatrephile* Vol. 2 no.5, Winter 84/85. The BBC Hulton Picture Library by David Lee.

THE BRITISH BROADCASTING CORPORATION includes the following libraries, all for staff use only:–
Drama Script Library (both radio and television)
Film Library
Gramophone Library
Photograph Library
Popular Music Library (catalogue now available on microfiche)
Recorded Programmes Library
Videotape Library

LONDON

109 BRITISH FILM INSTITUTE. Library

127 Charing Cross Road, London W1   (01) 437 4355

Hours	Tuesday–Wednesday 11–9, Thursday–Friday 11–6
Admission	Open to members
Contents	Book Library contains monographs on the theatre, theatre acting, theatre techniques and stage musicals.

Special Collections material (i.e. personal papers of individuals, organisations and companies involved in film and TV production). The following contain theatre material:-
Joseph Losey, Clive Brook, Will Hay, Douglas Sirk, Conrad Veidt.

Internal indexes Film and TV title (card index) includes details of film and TV versions of stage productions, opera and ballet.

Personality Card Index containing periodical references to film and TV directors, actors and technicians has some overlap with theatre. Also includes numerous references to Shakespeare on film and TV.

Subject Card Index includes periodical references to 'theatre and cinema' as a separate subject.

Book Library Catalogues On card. Alphabetical subject index, classified, author and title catalogues, personality and script catalogues.

see also
NATIONAL FILM ARCHIVE

LONDON

110 BRITISH LIBRARY

British Museum, Great Russell Street, London WC1B 3DG   (01) 636 1544

(a) REFERENCE DIVISION

Director General Alexander Wilson, FLA

Contact Reading Room for information on holdings. Ext. 209

Admission Free, by pass only. Applications must be made in writing to the Readers Admission Office, giving full name and permanent address, stating the specific purpose for which admission is required. Passes are normally available only to scholars over 21 years of age, who are following a specific line of research and who can establish that the material they wish to consult is unavailable elsewhere in London. The application must be accompanied by a written recommendation from a person of standing who has personal knowledge of the applicant. Day tickets are issued with slightly less formality. The pass gives access to a number of libraries within the Reference Division.

Hours Monday 9–5, Tuesday–Thursday 9–9, Friday–Saturday 9–5. (N.B. Readers to have left building by closing time)

Contents The library's collection of books was based on the library of Sir Hans Sloane (1660–1753), and on the Old Royal Library, and the Harleian and Cottonian Libraries. It is vigorously supplemented by the acquisition of antiquarian and current material from the UK and abroad. Copies of all works published in the UK have been required to be deposited, first at the Royal Library, then at the British Museum since 1662, although the effect of the acts was uncertain and discontinuous until the middle of the last century. This collection has been supplemented by the purchase and gift of complete libraries and individual items.

Material of special interest to the theatre historian includes:–

Archer, William. London and provincial theatre programmes, arranged alphabetically. 1895–1924. 7v. (Playbills 335-341)

Banks, Sophia Sarah. A collection of playbills, notices and press cuttings dealing with private theatrical performances. 1750–1808. (937.g.96)

Bulloch, John Malcolm. London and Aberdeen theatre programmes and newspaper cuttings relating thereto. With an index up to 1901. 1882–1938. 57v. (11797.c.1)

Burney, Charles. Collections of material relating to the theatre. (937.g.95-6; 938.a-f; 939.b.1,2; 939.d,e) Collections of playbills (937.b-e; 937.f.1,2; 937.g.96)

Chorley, John Rutter. Spanish dramatic literature, works relating to the Spanish drama and poetry. Presented 1867. (11726.h.9 and 11728.h.l-1.22)

Cox, Francis. 'Fragmenta'. A collection of parts of books, cuttings from newspapers, advertisements, playbills etc. 1788–1823. 94v. (937.g.1-94)

Daniel, George. A collection of illustrations, portraits, newspaper cuttings . . . manuscripts and playbills, relating principally to the Shakespeare Jubilee of 1769, and in particular to David Garrick's part therein. (C.61.e.2)

Evanion, Henry. A collection of pamphlets, handbills and misc. printed matter relating to theatres, fairs etc. 1800?–95. (Tab.11748.a)

Garrick, David. English drama: collection of play books of chiefly 16th and 17th centuries. (643.a-d; 644.a-l; C.34; C.21) Published catalogue available.

Gilbert, Sir William Schwenk. A collection of newspaper cuttings relating to W. S. Gilbert and the Savoy operas . . . 1879-1940. (Th.Cts.78)

Glynn, Hon. Sidney Carr. Playbills of London theatres. 1791–1895. 12v. (Playbills 352-363). Indexed in 'Register of playbills etc'. in Reading Room.

Gordon, Diana. English ballet, concert, opera and theatre programmes. Donated 1975. 1932–1974. (X.435/318) French, German and Italian concert, opera and theatre programmes . . . 1936–63. (X.431/2098)

Harris, Sir Augustus. A collection of newspaper cuttings relating to London theatres. 1704–1779. 6v (Th.Cts 1–6) A collection of playbills of Drury Lane Theatre from Oct. 1780 to March 1885. 45v. (Playbills 1–45)

Haslewood, Joseph. Of plays, players and play-houses, with other incidental matter. A collection of cuttings. 1703–1837. 9v. (11791.dd.18)

Lacy, Thomas Hailes. A collection of four copies of D. E. Baker 'Biographia dramatica', London 1812 with copious mss. notes and 6v of additions for a new edition. (11795.df. and k)

Larpent, John. MSS plays submitted to the Lord Chamberlain's Office 1737?–1824.; now in Henry H. Huntington Library, San Marino, California. Reproduced on opaque microcards in 'Three Centuries of English and American Plays'. N.Y. 1956. (Cup.700.1.1/ 6)

Northcott, Richard. A collection of libretti of operas ... with press cuttings, photos. c.1820–1940. (Northcott)

Percival, Richard. A collection relating to Sadler's Wells Theatre. 1683–1848. 14v. (Crach.1.Tab.4.b.4.)

Petherbridge, J. Covent Garden Opera programmes 1906–1939 inc. (Playbills 439–451, 453–467)

Russell,–. Foreign playbills 1845–56. (Playbills 303) London playbills 1847–1908 (Playbills 305); Provincial playbills 1845–1860 (Playbills 304)

Smith, Richard John. A collection of material towards a history of the English stage ... collected 1825?–40. 25v (11826.r,s)

Squire, William Barclay. London and foreign playbills and programmes, 1847–1919. (Playbills 342–7. 349–51). Indexed in 'Register of Playbills' in Reading Room.

Stoker, Bram. A collection, made by Bram Stoker, of programmes of theatrical performances with which Sir Henry Irving was connected. 1879–1905. (C.120.a.l and C.120.g.l)

Streatfeild, W. E. Theatrical notices from newspapers, with index. 1847–92. 28v. (Th.Cts.7–34)

Tieck, Johann Ludwig. A collection of books, mainly on drama, with mss. annotations. (C.182.a.l–b.l)

Turner, Dawson. A collection of ... playbills ... 1830–62 relating to Great Yarmouth. 9v. (1889.d.14) –Misc. material of local interest to Great Yarmouth.

Winston, James. A collection of memoranda, documents, playbills ... relating to Drury Lane Theatre from 1616 to 1830. 19 boxes. (C.120.h.l)

A series of scrapbooks relating to 18th and 19th century pleasure gardens is housed in the North Library.

Catalogues   The General Catalogue of Printed Books is available in university libraries and most public libraries. Updated catalogues are housed in the Reading Room.
N.B. Programmes are catalogued under the company managing the theatre.

Subject Index published to 1980.

Services   The Information Service is basically a bibliographical service; staff cannot undertake general research but can usually provide the names of professional researchers.

Photocopying service available, but subject to delays.

Material may be ordered in advance.

(b) DEPARTMENT OF MANUSCRIPTS

Keeper and Egerton Librarian D. P. Waley

Contact	The Students' Room
Admission	Free, by supplementary ticket issued in conjunction with pass for British Library Reader Admissions Office.
Hours	Monday–Saturday 10–4.45
Contents	Materials of interest to students of theatre history are scattered throughout the manuscript collections. They are traceable through the Department's published catalogues. Of particular interest are the three series of Lord Chamberlain's Plays: the first series covering the years 1824–1851 (Add. MSS 42865–43038) which is the subject of a special catalogue, the second series covering the years 1852–1899 (Add. MSS 52929–53708) and the third series covering the years 1900–1968. *These series contain printed as well as Ms. plays.

Since 1968 theatre managements have been required to deposit scripts of new plays with the department. These are being chased when not received.

Other major collections with a theatrical bias include the papers of George Bernard Shaw (Add. MSS 50508–50743) and of W. S. Gilbert (Add. MSS 49289–49353). This department also houses a vast collection of letters, including many from eminent playwrights, actors and actresses. There are also records relating to theatres, such as account books, leases and agreements.

Catalogues	A *Guide to the Catalogues and Indexes of the Dept. of Manuscripts* by M. A. E. Nickson 2nd ed. 1982. This contains a section on Play Collections. A more detailed survey of the collections and their catalogues will be found in T. C. Skeat's *The Catalogues of the Manuscript Collections,* revised edition, 1962.
Services	Photocopying available.
Notes	Manuscripts can be ordered in advance by writing direct to the Superintendent of the Reading Room 24 hours in advance.

*For plays submitted before 1824 *see under* Larpent, John in list of special collections under the Reference Division.

(c) NATIONAL SOUND ARCHIVE

see under

NATIONAL SOUND ARCHIVE — BRITISH LIBRARY

(d) NEWSPAPER LIBRARY

Colindale Avenue, London NW9 5HE   (01) 200 5515

Admission   As for Reference Division Reading Room. Passes issued at

Colindale are only valid for the Newspaper Library.

Hours	Monday–Saturday 10–5. Last application for material 4.15
Contents	The principal collection of newspapers within the British Library. It contains London newspapers from about 1801; Irish, Scottish, Welsh and English provincial newspapers from about 1700 on. Published indexes are held for *The Times, Financial Times* and *Glasgow Herald*. A large collection of Commonwealth newspapers and a representative collection of foreign newspapers. Newspapers in oriental languages are held by the Department of Oriental Printed Books and Manuscripts. The Indian Office Library and Records has impressive holdings of South Asian newspapers in the English language and is responsible for the collection of current English language newspapers from that area. Since 1973 the majority of United States west coast newspapers have been published on microfilm complete with their indexes.
Internal catalogues	Geographical sequence by place of publication, in loose-leaf volumes. An alphabetical title catalogue in a card cabinet.
Published catalogues	Printed catalogue published 1975 contains entries for British material to the end of 1970, overseas material to the end of 1971.
Services	Photocopying service available. Also microfilm copies of newspapers can be supplied, subject to copyright conditions.
Note	Newspaper searches cannot be undertaken. It is advisable to check that the items you wish to consult are available before travelling to Colindale.

LONDON

111   BRITISH MUSEUM. Department of Prints and Drawings

Great Russell Street, London WC1B 3DG   (01) 636 1555 Ext. 408

Keeper	J. K. Rowlands,
Contact	The Print Room
Admission	Regular users require a valid Student's Ticket
Hours	Monday–Friday 10–1, 2.15–4, Saturday 10–12.30
Contents	Drawings, watercolours and prints of stage settings, performances, costumes, theatrical personalities and buildings, dating from the 17th century, by English and continental artists. The department also has the Ralph Thomas Collection of Juvenile Drama.
Catalogues	Series of printed catalogues of the prints and drawings of each country. Also duplicated list of the most important theatrical material in the museum entitled *English School,* including foreign artists working in England, 17p.

Services	Photographic service available.
Note	Research must be undertaken by personal visit.

LONDON

112 BRITISH THEATRE ASSOCIATION

Currently 9 Fitzroy Square,London W1P 6AE   (01) 387 2666

From September 1986 Regents College, Inner Circle, Regents Park, London

Contact	Enid Foster, Librarian
Admission	Reference Library: Individual and corporate members of the association, on payment of the annual subscription, may have access to the reference facilities and information service, may borrow books and plays, hire play sets and books which can be sent through the post if required. Members receive the quarterly magazine *Drama*.
	British Theatre Play Library: Open to the public, by appointment.
Hours	Monday–Friday 10–5, Wednesday 10–7.30. By appointment.
Contents	Reference Library: The Library, the nucleus of which was provided in 1920 by Miss A. E. Horniman with manuscripts and annotated plays used during her tenancy of the Gaiety Theatre, Manchester, now has in excess of 250,000 volumes (some 50,000 titles). These cover all aspects of the drama and theatre arts, including plays. Extensive collection of indexed British and foreign theatre journals. Press cuttings from 1897 are updated daily and indexed.
	William Archer Collection: Theatre books including press cuttings and programmes from 1878 to 1924. Approximately 1,500 volumes.
	Harley Granville-Barker account book and press cuttings.
	Unity Theatre Archives.
	British Theatre Play Library: The Play Library has been available to members of the public for reference since 1983. The collection contains some 55,000 titles including published, and unpublished English plays, foreign plays in translation and in their original language. The collection is continually augmented by purchase and gift.
Indexes	Author, play title, subject indexes. Index to periodical articles. Plays are extensively catalogued, data includes date, publisher, cast, type of play, agent.
Editor's note	This major collection and information service is under threat due to withdrawal of grants. The move to Regents College is giving it a temporary reprieve but its future must be secured before the end of the decade.

LONDON

113   CAMDEN PUBLIC LIBRARIES. Hampstead and St. Pancras Local Collection

Swiss Cottage Library, 88 Avenue Road, London NW3 3HA

(01) 586 5984 Ext. 234 & 209

Contact	Local History Librarian, M. J. Holmes
Hours	Monday–Thursday 9.30–8, Saturday 9.30–5
Contents	Good collection of material on the Scala Theatre; items on Camden Theatre, Bedford Theatre, Hampstead Theatre Club, Shaw Theatre, and the Everyman Theatre, G. B. Shaw Collection.
Catalogue	Card
Guides to the collection	*Guide to the Collections.* 2nd ed. 1984 *Guide to London Local History Resources. London Borough of Camden,* Rev. ed. 1982 (neither list theatre material in detail)

LONDON

114   CAMDEN PUBLIC LIBRARIES. Holborn Local History Collection

Holborn Library, 32–38 Theobalds Road, London WC1X 8PA   (01) 430 1420
& (01) 405 2706

Contact	Local History Assistant
Hours	Monday–Thursday 9.30–8, Friday 9.30–6, Saturday 9.30–5
Contents	Material on Holborn Theatre, Holborn Amphitheatre, Holborn Empire, Kingsway Theatre, also Cambridge, Shaftesbury (previously Princes) and Saville Theatres.
Catalogues	Card

LONDON

115   CENTRAL SCHOOL OF ART AND DESIGN. Library

Southampton Row, London WC1B 4AP   (01) 405 1825

Contact	Ms S. M. Backemeyer
Admission	Reference only to personal visitors, by appointment. Loans can be arranged through British Library Lending Division.
Contents	Monographs and general material on theatre, its history and in particular stage design and lighting. Large collection of theatre periodicals. Microfiche of V. & A. Theatre Costumes Collection.
Internal catalogue	Microfiche.

LONDON
116 CENTRAL SCHOOL OF SPEECH AND DRAMA. Library

Embassy Theatre, Eton Avenue, London NW3 3H   (01) 722 8183

Contact	Angela Douglas
Admission	For reference purposes
Hours	Term time: Monday–Thursday 9–7, Friday 9–6 Vacations: Monday–Friday 9–6
Contents	Plays All aspects of theatre criticism, biographies, history Album of Edwardian theatre postcards New York Times Theatre Reviews 1870–1970 Theatre periodicals
Internal catalogues	Author and classified catalogues. Indexes to play reviews, plays in anthologies, and to people and subjects in theatre.

LONDON
117 CITY OF LONDON. Guildhall Library

Aldermanbury, London EC2P 2EJ   (01) 606 3030

(a) PRINT ROOM   Tel. Ext. 2839/2864

Hours	Monday–Friday 9.30–5
Contents	c.10,000 programmes and bills, chiefly London 19th century, filed by theatres. Several hundred prints, drawings and photographs of London theatres. Newscuttings and ephemera in the Noble Collection (box C28).
Catalogue	Card catalogue of prints and drawings.

(b) PRINTED BOOKS DEPARTMENT   Tel. Ext. 2868/2870

Hours	Monday–Saturday 9.30–5
Contents	Specialises in history and topography of England, especially London. Histories of London theatres. Biographies of actors and actresses. Approximately 1,600 mainly 19th century dramatic texts (Chapman and Hamilton Bequests). B. Pollock's juvenile dramas c.1840–1903. General reference works.
Catalogues	Author, general subject and London subject card catalogues.
Published catalogues	'Handlist of books in Guildhall Library on the London Theatre (1633–1900)' in Guildhall Miscellany Vol. 4 No. 2 April 1972

LONDON

118 The CITY UNIVERSITY. Department of Arts Policy and Management

Level 12,Frobisher Crescent, Barbican, Silk Street, London EC2Y 8HB
(01) 628 5641/2

Contact	Jane Purkiss (Departmental Administrator/Resource Administrator)
Hours	By arrangement
Contents	The Department Resources Centre contains a collection of periodicals, case studies, theses, dissertations, published reports and other publications relating to the administration of the arts. It is intended principally for students taking arts administration courses at The City University, but acess may be granted to other serious researchers. Apply in writing.
Catalogues	Card index by title and author, presently being updated on to DBase II.

LONDON

119 COVENT GARDEN ARCHIVES

The Royal Opera House, Covent Garden, London WC2

Contact	Francesca Franchi, Archivist
Admission	By written application only
Hours	Monday–Friday 10.30–1; 2.30–5
Contents	The Archives of the Royal Opera House aim to record the history of the three Covent Garden theatres, and all the people who have performed there, from 1732 to the present. For the first 150 years of its existence Covent Garden was a playhouse. The first theatre was destroyed by fire in 1808, and the second opened in 1809. This building was converted to an opera house in 1847, but destroyed by fire in 1856. The present building dates from 1858, and since 1946 has been the home of The Royal Ballet and The Royal Opera. The Royal Ballet was founded in 1931, as the Vic-Wells Ballet, and the Archives also try to cover the history of the company before its move to Covent Garden. The collection consists of a small reference library of books and periodicals (English and Foreign), press cuttings (mainly 20th century), 18th and 19th century prints, photographs, playbills, programmes and posters for performances at Covent Garden and also by The Royal Ballet and The Royal Opera on tour, some programmes from Drury Lane and other London theatres, and from foreign opera houses and ballet companies; costume and set designs (the collection includes c.1,100 costume designs by Attilio Comelli, designs by Cecil Beaton, Georges Wakhevitch, Salvador Dali, Leslie Hurry etc.), costumes, headdresses, jewellery, architectural plans, libretti, scores, correspondence, administrative records (some of which are

still confidential), colour slides, and tapes. The Archives has programmes and photos of foreign companies that have appeared at the Royal Opera House.

Internal indexes — Material is card-indexed under the name of the individual and under the title of the production, and cross-referenced. Some material is also listed under type-headings e.g. tapes, designs, slides, etc. Drama index complete; opera index virtually complete; ballet index in preparation.

LONDON
120 CUMING MUSEUM
155/157 Walworth Road, London SE17 1RS   (01) 703 3324/5529/6154

Contact — Museum Keeper

Hours — Monday–Friday 10–5.30, Thursday open until 7, Saturday 10–5

Contents — Includes model and plans of Tudor theatre, mementos of Stratford upon Avon and objects rescued from fire debris of Astley's Amphitheatre.

LONDON
121 DULWICH COLLEGE. Library
College Road, London SE21   (01) 693 3601

Contact — The Librarian

Admission — During term time, by appointment only. Written application should be made.

Contents — The archives of Edward Alleyn (1556–1626), the actor and founder of the school; and the account book and diary of Philip Henslowe (d.1616).

Catalogue — Published *Catalogue of the manuscripts and muniments of Alleyn's College of God's Gift at Dulwich*, 1881.

LONDON
122 EALING PUBLIC LIBRARIES. Local History Collection
Central Library, 103 Ealing Broadway Centre, The Broadway, London W5 5JY
(01) 567 3656

Contact — Miss Gooding

Hours — Monday closed, Tuesday 9–7.45, Wednesday 9–5, Thursday & Friday 9–7.45, Saturday 9–5

Contents — Material on the Questors Theatre at Ealing and Bankside Little Theatre. As yet uncatalogued. The department maintains an index to the *Middlesex County Times*, 1965 onwards.

LONDON

123　ENFIELD LIBRARIES. Local History Unit

Southgate Town Hall, Green Lanes, London N13　　　(01) 882 8841 Ext. 145

Contact　　　G. C. Dalling

Hours　　　　Monday–Saturday 9–5

Contents　　　Intimate Theatre, Palmers Green: press cuttings 1965+. Edmonton Empire: press cuttings. Amateur productions: playbills and programmes late 19th century on.

Indexes　　　General card index includes theatres and cinemas.

LONDON

124　ENGLISH HERITAGE (HISTORIC BUILDINGS & MONUMENTS COMMISSION FOR ENGLAND). London Division
formerly GREATER LONDON COUNCIL. Historic Buildings Division

Chesham House, 30 Warwick Street, London W1R 6AB　　(01) 734 8144 Ext. 13

Contact　　　Research Group

The division is responsible for the conversion of over thirty 'listed' theatre buildings in London and has built up a pool of knowledge and expertise on the architectural history of theatre building.

LONDON

125　GARRICK CLUB

Garrick Street, London WC2E 9AY　　　　　　　　　　(01) 836 1737

Contact　　　The Librarian

Admission　　To scholars, by appointment only. Fee £5, which may be increased if research is over a long period. Application should be made in writing to the Librarian, stating the subject of the research to be undertaken.

Contents　　　The Library of the Club was established in 1831 to serve the needs of its members. It houses approximately 5,000 play texts, 50 prompt books, 2,000 volumes on the theatre arts, 10,000 playbills and programmes from Drury Lane 1716 to date, 500 letters from Nell Gwyn onwards, and 50 periodical files including early 19th century titles. Generally strong on 18th and 19th century material. The Club also owns a large collection of theatrical paintings, many of which belonged to Charles Matthews (1776–1835) and his son. They depict the history of the British theatre from the 18th century.

Catalogues　　Card catalogue in the library. A *Catalogue of the Pictures in the Garrick Club* was published in 1936. A new catalogue is being prepared.

Service　　　No photocopying or microfilming is permitted.

Note　　　　Material may not be published in any form without permission in writing from the Library Committee.

LONDON

126 GREATER LONDON RECORD OFFICE AND HISTORY LIBRARY

40 Northampton Road, London EC1R 0HB   (01) 633 6851

Contact   Search Room, Miss J. Coburn, Head Archivist

Admission   No restrictions

Hours   Tuesday–Friday 10–4.45. Late opening Tuesday until 7.30, by appointment

Contents   The administrative records of the Greater London Council and its predecessors including the London County Council, Middlesex County Council and the Metropolitan Board of Works, 1855–1986.

The records include minutes, reports and papers of successive Theatres and Music Halls Committees, Entertainments (licensing) Committees and Public Control Committees, plus fire reports of the Metropolitan Fire Brigade. The records of the Middlesex Sessions from 1549 contain innumerable references to crime and the theatre, as well as records of the records of the granting of music and dancing licences from the 18th century.

The Record Office has in addition a large number of uncatalogued playbills and programmes, as well as prints and photographs.

The office holds theatre plans for approx. 1,600 premises.

Catalogues   Card catalogues and handlists. Card index to theatre plans arranged alphabetically by name of theatre.

Services   Photography, microfilming and photocopying services are available, dependent on the nature of the material.

Note   The staff cannot undertake long and detailed research on behalf of enquiries.

Greater London Council. Building Regulation Division Records:
The responsibilities of this department included the inspection of premises licensed as places of entertainment to ensure safety standards were maintained. In the course of this work Theatre Cases were built up which gave a complete history of the structure of the building, and included plans and elevations which were redrawn at approx. 10-year intervals. Information collected included the accommodation provided by theatres, facilities for invalids, means of escape, types of dressing rooms, ratio of stage to auditorium area etc.

The catalogues included a 2 volume case record 1903–c.1940, plus a card index.

This material is currently held in the Record Office in County Hall. Its future location is undecided. Enquiries should be made to the Greater London Record Office at 40 Northampton Road, above.

LONDON

127 GREENWICH PUBLIC LIBRARIES. Local History Library

Woodlands, 90 Mycenae Road, London SE3 7SE

Contact	Local History Librarian
Hours	Monday, Tuesday and Thursday 9–8, Saturday 9–5
Contents	Material on most theatres in the Greenwich and Woolwich area, items cover period 18th century to present day.
Catalogue	Card and indexes.

LONDON

128 GUNNERSBURY PARK MUSEUM

Gunnersbury Park, London W3 8LQ   (01) 992 1612

Contact	P. Philo, Curator
Hours	November–February: Monday–Friday 1–4, Saturday, Sunday and Bank Holidays 2–4 March–October: Monday–Friday 1–5, Saturday, Sunday and Bank Holidays 2–6
Contents	Small collection of 19th century playbills and programmes relating to London theatres. Programmes for Chiswick Empire, 1920s, 30s and 1950s. Newspaper cuttings relating to local amateur groups.
Indexes	Indexes to references in newspaper cuttings, reference books, and general ephemera collections.

LONDON

129 HACKNEY PUBLIC LIBRARIES. Archives Department

Rose Lipman Library, De Beauvoir Road, London N1 5SQ   (01) 241 2886

Contact	Archivist: D. L. Minder or any member of the staff
Admission	By appointment only
Hours	Monday 10–8, Tuesday–Friday 10–5.30, Saturday 10–1, 2–5
Contents	Printed texts of Buckstone melodramas. 960 playbills and programmes for 1840–1880. Letters, prints and photographs. The playbills are from the City of London Theatre, the Standard, the Grecian, and the Britannia. Also theatre sheets and characters produced by Pollocks Toy Theatres.
Indexes	Certain items, including the letters, are part of the Archive collection and catalogued and indexed in the archive lists and subject index. The playbills are not catalogued, but have been microfilmed in order of theatre and then by date of playbill, and the microfilm is normally used by the public. All other items are in the local history library catalogue, which has subject/title and classified indices.

Catalogues   Archive: typescript lists, card subject index, card index of persons. Local history: card catalogues.

LONDON

130   HAMMERSMITH AND FULHAM PUBLIC LIBRARIES.
Archives Collection

7 Uxbridge Road, London W12   (01) 743 0910

Contact   Borough Archivist

Hours   Monday and Friday 9.15–5, Tuesday and Thursday 9.15–8

Contents   Letter books and cash books of the Kings Theatre 1901–1940.

LONDON

131   HAMMERSMITH AND FULHAM PUBLIC LIBRARIES.
Fulham Local History Collection

56 Fulham Road, London SW6 5NX   (01) 736 1127/8

Contact   Local History Librarian

Hours   Monday, Tuesday, Thursday 9.15–8, Friday and Saturday 9.15–5. Closed all day Wednesday. (Appointment advisable)

Contents   Material, including a collection of photographs, on the Grand Theatre, Granville Theatre and Bishops Park Open Air Theatre.

LONDON

132   HAMMERSMITH AND FULHAM PUBLIC LIBRARIES.
Hammersmith Local History Collection

Central Library, Shepherds Bush Road, London W6   (01) 748 6032

Contact   Local History Librarian

Hours   Monday, Tuesday, Thursday 9.15–8, Friday and Saturday 9.15–5. Closed all day Wednesday.

Contents   Material on Hammersmith Palace of Varieties, Kings Theatre and Lyric Opera House, Shepherds Bush Empire and other local theatres.

LONDON

133   IMPERIAL WAR MUSEUM. Department of Documents and Printed Books

Lambeth Road, London SE1 6HZ   (01) 735 8922

Contact   R. W. A. Suddaby, Keeper of Dept. of Documents
              Dr G. M. Bayliss, Keeper of Dept. of Printed Books

Admission   By appointment

Hours   Monday–Friday 10–5

Contents   **The Department of Printed Books:**
has a substantial collection of books, pamphlets and programmes relating to civilian and forces entertainments during the two World Wars and other conflicts of the 20th century.

The Department of Documents:
holds a collection of private papers of Mrs Virginia Vernon which consists of letters, diaries, notebooks, reports and miscellaneous documents relating to her service with ENSA, mainly as Chief ENSA Welfare Officer, January 1940–June 1946, and dealing with the travel and accommodation arrangements and other welfare matters for entertainers working for ENSA in France, the Middle East, Italy, India, Burma, and with the B.L.A. in Northern Europe. Included in the collection is correspondence with Basil Dean, January 1944–January 1946.

LONDON

134 ISLINGTON PUBLIC LIBRARIES.
Finsbury Local History Collection

Finsbury Library, 245 St. John Street, London EC1V 4NB   (01) 837 4161

Contact   Reference Librarian, David Whithey

Admission   Appointment only

Hours   Monday, Tuesday and Thursday 9–8, Wednesday and Friday 9–1, Saturday 9–5

Contents   The Sadler's Wells Collection. This is one of the largest collections of material in London on an individual theatre; it includes 130 prompt books, approx. 2,000 playbills and programmes, approx. 3,000 press cuttings and 150 prints. The collection is un-catalogued.

The Sadler's Wells Theatre has now transferred its archives here. Material in process of listing.

LONDON

135 ISLINGTON PUBLIC LIBRARIES.
Islington Local History Collection

Central Library, 68 Holloway Road, London N7 (01) 609 3051 Ext. 31 or 33

Contact   Principal Reference Librarian, Valerie Dawson

Hours   Monday–Friday 9–8, Saturday 9–5

Contents   Small collection of material on Collin's Music Hall, the Grand Theatre, Islington Empire, and Kings Head. Particularly strong on 20th century material.

Contents Material on the Deptford Theatre, Lewisham Hippodrome and New Cross Empire.

LONDON
136 KENSINGTON AND CHELSEA PUBLIC LIBRARIES.
Chelsea Local History Collection

Chelsea Library, Old Town Hall, King's Road, London SW3   (01) 352 6056

Contact   Reference Librarian

Admission   Appointment preferred

Hours   Monday, Tuesday, Thursday 10–8, Friday 10–5, Wednesday 10–1, Saturday 10–5

Contents   Material on the Chelsea Palace and Royal Court Theatres.

LONDON
137 KENSINGTON AND CHELSEA PUBLIC LIBRARIES.
Kensington Local History Collection

Central Library, Phillimore Walk, London W8   (01) 937 2542

Contact   Local History Librarian

Admission   Appointment preferred

Hours   Monday, Tuesday, Thursday and Friday 10–8, Wednesday 10–1, Saturday 10–5

Contents   A few items of the Mercury Theatre, Bolton's Theatre Club, Century/Bijou Theatre and Coronet Theatre.

LONDON
138 LAMBETH PUBLIC LIBRARIES.
Lambeth Archives Dept. (Surrey Collection)

Minet Library, 52 Knatchbull Road, London SE5 9QY   (01) 733 3279

Contact   Borough Archivist, Mrs P. Hatfield

Admission   By appointment

Hours   Monday–Friday & alternate Saturdays 9.30–1, 2–5, closed Wednesday

Contents   Lambeth and Surrey topography. Large collections of playbills, photographs, prints and press cuttings on Surrey Theatre, Bower Saloon, Surrey Zoological Gardens, Astleys, and the Old Vic. Extensive collection of material on Vauxhall Gardens.

Catalogue   Card

LONDON
139 LEWISHAM PUBLIC LIBRARIES. Local History Department
The Manor House, Old Road, London SE13 5SY   (01) 852 5050

| Contact | C. Harrison, Archivist |
| Hours | Tuesday & Thursday 9.30–8, Monday/Friday/Saturday 9.30–5. Closed Wednesday. |

LONDON
140   LORD CHAMBERLAIN'S OFFICE
St. James's Palace, London SW1

The Lord Chamberlain's Office archives contained manuscripts of plays submitted for license from 1900 to 1968, irrespective of whether or not a licence was actually granted. The manuscripts have been transferred to the British Library, where they are available for inspection and where copies may be made on payment of a fee. The Library rules require a researcher to sign the copyright disclaimer, since many of the scripts are still in copyright and may not be reproduced without the holder's permission. The relevant correspondence has been retained at St. James's Palace as part of the Office records and is not open to inspection. However, access has been given to researchers in the past and applications should be made in writing to the Secretary of the Office.

LONDON
141   MERTON PUBLIC LIBRARIES.
Wimbledon Local History Collection

Wimbledon Reference Library, Wimbledon Hill Road, London SW19

(01) 946 1136

Contact	Reference Library
Hours	Monday, Tuesday, Thursday, Friday 9–7, Wednesday and Saturday 9–5
Contents	Some programmes and playbills for the Wimbledon Theatre, 1945 onwards; publications of the Friends of Wimbledon Theatre,1969 onwards; press cuttings on amateur theatre in the area, 1911–1923.
Note	The Wimbledon Reference Library is transferring to Morden in 1987. Contact (01) 545 3771 for details.

LONDON
142   MUSEUM OF LONDON
London Wall, London EC2Y 5HN

(01) 600 3699

Contact	Initial enquiries to Nicola Johnson, Curator of Printed Ephemera.
Admission	Appointments may be made to see items not on exhibition.
Contents	The Museum covers all aspects of the history of London. Items of interest to theatre researchers include costumes, stage jewellery and properties of performers in most forms of entertainments.

Special collections include prompt books and costumes of Sir Henry Irving, the Martin Harvey Collection of material on his productions and miscellaneous items ranging from the front door of Astley's to the envelope on which Albert Chevalier wrote 'My dear Old Dutch'.

In the collection of printed ephemera are playbills, programmes and scrapbooks of London theatres, music halls and pleasure gardens and the Jonathan King Collection of Juvenile Drama.

LONDON

143 NATIONAL FILM ARCHIVE

81 Dean Street, London W1V 6AA   (01) 437 4355

Contact	David Francis, Curator
Admission	Free to bonefide enquirers. Where duplicate prints exist, viewings for the purpose of study and research can be arranged, though limited viewing facilities result in a waiting list.
Contents	80,000 films and TV programmes covering features, documentaries and newsreels shown in Great Britain, irrespective of their country of origin, from 1895 (the inception of film). The collection does not contain film of stage productions, but it does include many notable theatrical figures in film productions, e.g. Forbes-Robertson in *Hamlet* (1913). The Archive's collection of newsreels contains film of stage personalities, including Sarah Bernhardt and Ellen Terry. Also film of music hall performers from Little Titch onwards. Some films and videotapes of television drama and television documentaries about theatre productions. Stills Collection from feature films contains photographs of theatre personalities. (Contact Michelle Snapes for appointment.)
Catalogue	Collection indexed under titles, film directors, subjects and casts. Title catalogue in visible index record books, other indexes on cards.

LONDON

144 NATIONAL MONUMENT RECORD. ROYAL COMMISSION ON HISTORICAL MONUMENTS (ENGLAND)

Fortress House, 23 Savile Row, London W1X 1AB   (01) 734 6010

Secretary	Dr Peter Fowler
Admission	Free
Hours	Monday–Friday 10–5.30
Contents	Measured drawings and c.1 million photographs of archaeological sites and buildings of architectural and historic interest in England, including many theatres. Department of the Environment Statutory Lists of Buildings of Historical and

Architectural Importance are held for England.
Service   Photographic service available.

LONDON

145 NATIONAL OPERATIC AND DRAMATIC ASSOCIATION. Library

1 Crestfield Street, London WC1H 8AU   (01) 837 5655

Contact   The Librarian

Hours   Monday–Friday 10–4

The Association was founded in 1899. The Library exists to serve its members and is only of interest to those involved with light musical theatre.

Contents   Vocal scores, libretti, and about 2,000 general works are available to members. Some items may only be examined on the premises.

Catalogue   Card

Service   Information service. Advice for members only.

LONDON

146 NATIONAL PORTRAIT GALLERY

St. Martin's Place, London WC2H 0HE   (01) 930 1552

Director   John Hayes

Hours   Monday–Friday 10–5, Saturday 10–6, Sunday 2–6

Contents   The national collection of portraits in all media, including theatrical personalities from Shakespeare and Jonson onwards.

Indexes   Internal — Under sitters, artists, photographs and locations.

Catalogues   Internal — Card catalogue to NPG collections.
                Published 'Complete Illustrated Catalogue 1856–1979'. Catalogue raisonnes in print: Tudor and Jacobean, Seventeenth Century and Early Victorian.

Services   Photographic service available. Information service — the staff will assist serious enquirers to locate portraits in other collections.

Note   Portraits are loaned for exhibition, subject to the approval of the Trustees.

LONDON

147 NATIONAL PORTRAIT GALLERY ARCHIVE AND LIBRARY

15 Carlton House Terrace, London SW1Y 5AH   (01) 930 1552

Admission   By appointment only

Hours   Monday–Friday 10–5

Contents   Photographic record of portraits in all media, covering mainly

British subjects, and from collections other than the NPG. A reference collection of engravings and original photographs, including theatrical personalities. Library of books on all aspects of portraiture, only open to researchers as library of last resort.

Indexes   Internal — Card index filed by name of sitter, giving information which supplements that in the picture library.

Catalogues   Internal — Card catalogue to the library.

'Dictionary of British Portraiture' by Adriana Davies and Elaine Kilmurray, 4 vols. Batsford. (Based on Archive collections and records) 1979–81

LONDON

148   NATIONAL SOUND ARCHIVE — BRITISH LIBRARY

29 Exhibition Road, London SW7 2AS   (01) 589 6603/6604

Contact   Curator of Recorded Literature

Admission   The Archive provides a free playback service to any member of the public. Groups from schools and other institutions up to fifty in number, by prior arrangement. It is advisable to make an appointment by telephone, or by writing to 'The Public Playback Service'.

Hours   Monday–Friday 10.30–5.30, Thursday 10.30–9

Contents   More than 400,000 discs of all kinds and over 20,000 hours of recorded tape. Within the collection there is a unique library of plays.

Productions include: RSC London seasons at Aldwych and Barbican 1964–. Peter Daubeny's World Theatre seasons at Aldwych 1964–75. National Theatre Company from opening production of 'Hamlet' at the Old Vic 1963–. Royal Court Theatre 1972–. Traverse Theatre, Edinburgh (selected productions) 1970–. Edinburgh Festival (selected items) 1981–

Also selected productions of: Manchester Royal Exchange, Bristol Old Vic, Edinburgh Royal Lyceum, Chichester Festival Theatre, Riverside Studios, Arts Theatre.

Commercial material: Many published UK productions from cylinders to compact disc, plus a wide range of foreign language productions.

Radio plays: All BBC Transcription and Sound Archive recordings dating back to the earliest radio drama productions. A number of Independent Radio plays are also available.

An oral history of the RSC in Stratford has been compiled.

Theatre programmes: Alphabetical file (under title) of programmes from all NSA live theatre productions.

Catalogues   Card catalogue available to the public covers most plays in the collection, giving author / title / cast / characters / producer /

76

composer / date / place / recording details / retrieval number.

The NSA Reference Library contains BBC Catalogues, plus BBC/ Chadwyck-Healey Fiche of BBC Drama, which gives access to NSA holdings of BBC material.

Record catalogues from commercial producers dating back to the beginning of the century are card-indexed, as is the large collection of discographies.

Note   *Theatrephile* Vol. 2, no.6, Spring 1985. The National Sound Archive: the collection of theatre recordings, by Jonathan Vickers.

LONDON
149   NEWHAM PUBLIC LIBRARIES. Local Studies Library
Stratford Reference Library, Water Lane, London E15 4NJ
                              (01) 534 4545 Ext. 5662 (office hours)
                              (01) 534 1305 (evenings and Saturdays)

Contact   Local Studies Librarian, H. Bloch

Admission   Appointment necessary

Hours   Monday, Tuesday, Wednesday, Friday 9.30–7, Thursday 2–7, Saturday 9.30–5

Contents   Collection of material on the Theatre Royal, Stratford, consisting of programmes relating to the Theatre Workshop Group and to the theatre itself prior to World War I. A history of the theatre, privately published 1962, together with a manuscript index is available.

                The Theatre Royal, Stratford, is in the process of depositing its archives with the library, and a catalogue and indexes will be produced c.1985 when deposit arrangements are completed.

LONDON
150   PASSMORE EDWARDS MUSEUM
Romford Road, Stratford, London E15 4LZ   (01) 519 4296
                            and (01) 534 4545 Ext. 5670

Contact   Mrs Barbara Colla

Hours   Monday–Friday 10–6, Saturday 10–5, Sundays & Bank Holidays 2–5.

Contents   *The Archives of the British Music Hall Society Collection have been housed here since 1985. The Collection includes photographic material, showcards, posters from theatres in London, Brighton and Edinburgh. Costume items belonging to famous music hall artistes such as Vesta Tilley's waistcoat, Bud Flanagan's coat and Max Miller's suit.

Note   *Collection not on public display at present.

Indexes   Index in progress.

LONDON

152 PUBLIC RECORD OFFICE

Keeper	G. H. Martin
Admission	Free, by ticket obtainable from office
Contact	Enquiry desks
Hours	Monday–Friday 9.30–5
Catalogues	The Search Rooms house typescript calendars of each department.

(a) Chancery Lane, London WC2   (01) 405 0751

Lord Chamberlain's Office, Class LC7 1660–1901:
These are contained in 89 volumes, portfolios etc. and include warrants, registers of licences, inspection reports, plans of theatres, etc.
LC1 1710–1902:
775 volumes containing the correspondence of the Office of the Lord Chamberlain who is the licenser of theatres in and about the centre of London and at Windsor, and who was the licenser of all stage plays.

There is also theatre information in the State Papers Domestic, the Exchequer Records and the Privy Council Records, and in the records of legal proceedings.

(b) Ruskin Avenue, Kew, Richmond, Surrey   (01) 876 3444

Board of Trade papers. Records, reports etc. on limited companies.
Home Office papers. (H.O. 179) 1910–1921. 1 v. relate to licensing, safety precautions etc.
Law Officers Miscellaneous Reports (H.O. 119) 1792–1870. 18 v. includes material on theatre disputes of 1816–18.
Works Department (Miscellaneous Works 6) 1609–1951. 401 v. includes material on the King's Theatre Haymarket 1828–29.

LONDON

153 PUPPET CENTRE TRUST

Battersea Arts Centre, Lavender Hill, London SW11   (01) 228 5335

Contact	The Administrator
Library	The centre has its own library which is available to the public. Its stock includes a collection of standard works of reference, an illustrations collection (posters and photographs), newspaper clippings, and a collection of British and foreign journals.
Services	Information service — Freely available to anyone. Research is not usually undertaken, but help will be given to those undertaking research. Photocopy service available.

Note　　Apart from the knowledge and experience of the staff and the resources of the library, contact is maintained with professionals and experts in the field; these contacts provide an important information resource.

LONDON

154　RAYMOND MANDER AND JOE MITCHENSON THEATRE COLLECTION

5 Venner Road, Sydenham, London SE26　　　　　　　　(01) 778 6730

Contact　　Colin Mabberley, Curator

Admission　By appointment only

Contents　The collection, one of the most extensive in the country, includes material on all aspects of the theatre, and contains many playbills, programmes, prints and photographs, as well as museum items.

Note　　Widely used as a source of illustrations and information by the broadcasting media, publishers etc., the collection is now a registered charitable trust, and is currently being moved to Beckenham Place Park, in Beckenham, by arrangement with the London Borough of Lewisham.

LONDON

155　ROYAL ACADEMY OF DRAMATIC ART

62–64 Gower Street, London WC1E 6EW　　　　　　　　(01) 636 7076

(a) Library

Contact　　Clare Hope

Admission　By appointment only

Hours　　Term time only: Tuesday, Thursday, Friday 11–7

Contents　50 per cent of 11,000 vol. stock is play texts.
Also theatre biographies, history and criticism, and material on acting, costume, stage fights, makeup, directing, stage management and stage design.

(b) The Ivo Curall Shaw Collection

Contact　　Richard O'Donoghue

Admission　By written application only

Contents　450 books by G. B. Shaw or to which he has contributed, and on Shaw. The collection includes pamphlets and tracts.

(c) RADA Archives

Contact　　Richard O'Donoghue (Administrator-Registrar)

Admission　By written application only

Contents　Records of students from 1904. Name only until 1920s, after which the records become more detailed.

LONDON

156 ROYAL INSTITUTE OF BRITISH ARCHITECTS.
Drawings Collection

21 Portman Square, London W1H 9HF   (01) 580 5533

Contact	John Harris, Curator
Admission	By appointment
Hours	Monday–Friday 10–1 (Tel. enquiries received from 10 am)
Contents	The Institute's collection of 250,000 architectural drawings, from the 16th century onward, contains a considerable number on theatre buildings and stage sets by English and continental architects, including works by Palladio, Inigo Jones, Juvarra, and the Galli Bibiena Family.
Catalogue	Card catalogue and subject index. General catalogue, arranged alphabetically under architect, is in the process of publication.

LONDON

157 SIR JOHN SOANE'S MUSEUM

13 Lincoln's Inn Fields, London WC2   (01) 405 2107

Contact	Peter Thornton, Curator Miss Dorothy Stroud, Inspectress and Assistant Curator
Hours	Tuesday–Saturday 10–5; Closed Bank Holidays
Contents	A miscellaneous collection which includes a few items of interest to theatre historians, notably architectural drawings of Italian and English Theatres.
Catalogue	Ledgers available for inspection at the museum.
Service	Photographic service arranged through a photographic firm.
Note	Students requiring access to the drawings are advised to make an appointment.

LONDON

158 SOUTHWARK PUBLIC LIBRARIES. Local Studies Library

John Harvard Library, 211 Borough High Street, London SE1 1JA
                                                       (01) 403 3507

Contact	Local Studies Librarian
Hours	Monday and Thursday 9.30–8, Tuesday and Friday 9.30–5, Saturday 9.30–1. By appointment only. The collection closes 12.30–1.30
Contents	Histories, playbills, programmes, cuttings and illustrations on theatres and music halls in Southwark and adjacent areas, especially Astley's, South London Palace, Rosemary Branch, Surrey Gardens and Surrey Theatre.
	Collection of secondary sources on the Globe and other

Elizabethan theatres on Bankside.

Catalogues Internal — General author and subject catalogue to printed books and pamphlets includes brief entries for works on local theatres.

LONDON

159 The SPOTLIGHT

42/43 Cranbourn Street, London WC2H 7AP (01) 437 7631

Admission Available to members of the theatre profession

Hours Hours 10–5.30

Contents Publishers of *Spotlight*, the casting directory, and *Contacts*. This organisation provides the most comprehensive information service on the professional theatre. Detailed records are kept for actors and actresses, giving full data on their dialectic ability, languages, physical attributes etc. and these are cross-referenced. Agent's address and current working address is also recorded. Information is held on all members of the theatrical profession (but not on members of the other live performing arts such as opera, variety etc.) regardless of whether they choose to advertise or not. Records are constantly updated and new entrants into the profession are interviewed while at drama school. Owing to work-permit difficulties these records relate to UK nationals, although data is kept on international stars. In addition records are kept on directors, designers, etc., and on repertory companies, theatre buildings and arts centres.

A file of programmes has been maintained since the 1930s.

LONDON

160 THEATRE MUSEUM

Victoria and Albert Museum, Cromwell Road, London SW7 2RL

(01) 589 6371

The new museum is due to open in the Old Flower Market, Covent Garden (beneath the London Transport Museum) in the Spring of 1987.

Curator Alexander Schouvaloff

Admission Details to be announced

Contents The Victoria and Albert Museum's Theatre Section, the collection dates back to 1925 when Mrs Gabrielle Enthoven gave her collection of programmes and playbills to the V & A. Since the Theatre Museum was opened in 1974 major collections have continued to be added to the individual items acquired by the section through purchase and gift.

Outstanding collections given to the Theatre Section are those of Gabrielle Enthoven, Harry R. Beard and the Friends of the Museum of Performing Arts.

The Gabrielle Enthoven Theatre Collection: Donated by its creator in 1924. Mrs Enthoven followed up this gift by twenty five years' personal work and then by a bequest in 1950, entitled the Gabrielle Enthoven Theatre Collection Fund, for the purchase of major items as they became available. This collection includes over one million playbills, programmes and related material on the London stage from 1718; since 1925, with the cooperation of the London theatre managers this has become a comprehensive collection.

The Harry R. Beard Collection: Bequeathed to the Theatre Section in 1971, the collection was started in 1939, and, by the time of the founder's death, had achieved the size of a major theatre museum in its own right. It is chiefly important for the wealth of early French and Italian designs and engravings, and for the extensive collections of material on the 18th and early 19th centuries. In its coverage it is complementary to the Enthoven Collection.

Friends of the Museum of Performing Arts Collection: comprises a major collection of ballet material relating to Diaghilev productions.

In addition there are approximately forty major collections including:– Collection of stage designs and models given by the Arts Council of Great Britain and the British Council. Huston Rogers Collection of Photographs (1930s–50s). Rock and Pop costume and memorabilia. Ashley Dukes-Marie Rambert Collections of Engraved Prints of the ballet. The London Archives of the Dance. The Guy Little Theatrical Photograph Collection 1857–90. The Andrew Melville Collection of Melodramas. The Nancy Price Collection of production records and playscripts. The Hinkins Collection of Toy Theatre. The M. W. Stone Collection of Juvenile Drama. The C. B. Cochran Productions Newspaper Archive. The Sydney Carroll Collection of Newspaper and Periodical Cuttings 1920–1939. The Anthony Hippisley Coxe Circus Collection. Vic-Wells Association Collection on Sadler's Wells and the Old Vic (under deposit).

The scope of the material available in the Theatre Museum:– photographs c.1855 onwards; playbills and programmes 1718 onwards; all forms of prints and engravings depicting scenes from plays, and portraits; manuscript letters, receipts and accounts etc. c1700+, theatre plans, original designs for scenes and costumes from the 16th century to date.

Files of press cuttings, programmes and related material are arranged under the name of the theatre, in date order.

Biographical material, once filed with theatres, is now being extracted into a separate sequence.

Note	Materials not on display in the exhibition areas at Covent Garden, will, where possible, be made available to researchers in the Students Room which has approx. 15 places.

Theatre Museum Reference Library

Contents	Periodicals of the 18th and 19th centuries, and complete runs of most 20th century periodicals relating to the theatre. Theatre biography, play-texts, prompt books, libretti, histories and works of reference.
Catalogue	Typed catalogue of original designs, posters etc. Card index of remainder.
Note	Extensive research on behalf of enquirers cannot be undertaken. Some catalogues and indexes are several years in arrears, and the location of later material depends on the knowledge of the staff.

LONDON

161   TOWER HAMLETS PUBLIC LIBRARIES. Local History Library

Central Library, 277 Bancroft Road, London E1 4DQ   (01) 980 4366

Hours	Monday–Friday 9–8, Wednesday and Saturday 9–5, (appointment advisable)
Contents	Material, mainly cuttings and illustrations, on the People's Palace, Pavilion Theatre, Whitechapel and other Stepney theatres, especially the Royalty Theatre and Garrick Theatre, and also the Queen's Theatre, Poplar.
Catalogue	Internal — Classified catalogue, theatres separated into Bethnal Green, Poplar and Stepney areas.

LONDON

162A   UNIVERSITY OF LONDON LIBRARY

Senate House, Malet Street, London WC1E 7HU   (01) 636 4514

Contact	Director of Central Library Services and Goldsmiths Librarian
Admission	Members of the university. Non-members who can show a particular need, during vacations, by written application.
Hours	Term time: Monday–Thursday 9.30–9, Friday 9.30–6.30, Saturday 9.30–5.30. Easter Vacation: as above. Summer and Christmas Vacations: Monday–Saturday 9.30–5.30
Contents	General university library stock.
Note	The Malcolm Morley Collection and the library of the Society for Theatre Research are deposited here on a temporary basis.
Contact	Miss D. Proctor (Tuesdays and Thursdays)

LONDON

162B VICTORIA AND ALBERT MUSEUM

South Kensington, London SW7 2RL   (01) 589 6371

Director	Dr Roy Strong,
Exhibition Galleries open	Monday–Saturday 10-6, Sunday 2.30-5.30. Closed Friday

Opened on 22 June 1857, the museum has developed from a proposal of the Select Committee on the Arts and Manufactures in 1835. Formerly known as the Museum of Manufactures, it originally opened at Marlborough House in 1852.

The departments of primary interest to the theatre researcher are the Library and the Department of Prints, Drawings and Paintings; the Department of Textiles with its extensive collection of costumes and fabrics, and the Department of Woodwork, with its collection of period furniture and interior decoration, are of considerable interest to the designer.

(a) The Art Library

Contact	Library enquiries
Admission	Free for regular users holding a library ticket issued by the V. & A. Library or the British Library.
Hours	Monday–Thursday 10-5.45, Saturday 10-1, 2-5.45. Closed Friday
Contents	Includes thousands of items on the history of the theatre arts, and on design in general. It also contains the collections of literature donated in the 19th century by Alexander Dyce and John Forster, which includes the works of many English dramatists of the 16th and 17th centuries; plus 40 volumes of the correspondence of David Garrick, and the Piot Collection of books on 17th, 18th and 19th century spectacle.
Catalogues	General catalogue in Guard Book form. Subject index. Portrait index.
Service	Photocopying service available.
Note	It is not possible for the staff to undertake detailed research on behalf of enquirers.

(b) Department of Prints, Drawings & Photographs, and Prints

Keeper	Michael Kauffmann
Hours	Monday–Thursday 10-4.30. Saturday 10-1 and 2-4.30
Contents	The department houses approximately one million items. The subject matter is wide ranging.
Catalogues	Artists, topographical, subject and portrait indexes, in book, card and sheaf forms respectively.

Published guides	*Handbook to the Department of Prints, Drawings & Photographs, and Paintings* 2nd ed. 1983.
Services	Photographic service available; personal cameras and equipment can be used by prior arrangement.
Note	Material is loaned for exhibition purposes, subject to the approval of the Keeper.

LONDON

163   WANDSWORTH PUBLIC LIBRARIES.
Battersea Local History Collection

265 Lavender Hill, London SW11   (01) 871 7467

Contact	Tony Shaw, Local History Librarian
Hours	Wednesday and Friday 10–5, Tuesday 10–8, Saturday by appointment
Contents	A few items on the Battersea Palace Theatre. 7 programmes. Balham Hippodrome (Duchess Theatre) 1910–1914.

LONDON

164   WESTFIELD COLLEGE (UNIVERSITY OF LONDON).
Caroline Skeel Library

Kidderpore Avenue, Hampstead NW3 7ST   (01) 435 7141

Contact	Mrs M. E. Helyar, Assistant Librarian
Admission	Available for consultation during library opening hours. For extended use, the Librarian's permission must be obtained.
Hours	Term time: Monday–Friday 9–9, Saturday 9–5 Vacations: Monday–Friday 9–5
Contents	Book collection of play texts and works on drama and theatre to support undergraduate courses. Play sets deposited by the British Theatre Association. Major subject areas covered by books and periodicals index: Drama and theatre of English, French, Spanish and United States, and to a lesser extent, classical, Italian, German and Latin American theatre and drama.
Catalogue	Internal — Card catalogue of book collection. Card index by subject of articles on drama and theatre in approximately 90 periodicals.

LONDON

165   WESTMINSTER CITY LIBRARIES. Central Reference Library

St. Martin's Street, London WC2H 7HP   (01) 828 8074

Telex	261845
Contact	Head of Reference Services
Hours	Monday–Friday 10–7, Saturday 10–5

Contents	Includes Special Collection on the Performing Arts, including bibliographies, major works of reference, memoirs, histories etc.

(Editor: This major collection of published material on the theatre is unique in London, being both freely available and readily accessible.)

LONDON

166 WESTMINSTER CITY LIBRARIES.
Westminster Archives and Local History Collection (Marylebone)
Marylebone Library, Marylebone Road, London NW1 5PS
(01) 828 8070 Ext. 4030

Contact	Archivist
Hours	Monday–Friday 9.30–7, Saturday 9.30–1, 2–5
Contents	Princess's Theatre, Oxford Street:

    c.600 playbills 1840–1902 including 4 bound volumes October 1848–June 1849, October 1849–May 1850, January 1843–December 1854, January 1855–October 1874

West London Theatre, Church Street:
    c.350 playbills 1832–1912 and other material

Oxford Theatre:
    bound volumes of programmes 1879–80, 1882–89

Queen's Hall, Langham Place:
    60 programmes 1895–1938

Printed material, newscuttings, prints and photographs are also available which relate to these theatres. Smaller groups of material are held for:
    The Royal Sussex Theatre, Bell Street and The Metropolitan Theatre, Edgware Road

Indexes	Internal — Indexes to Paddington, St. Marylebone and the Ashbridge Collection (which relates to St. Marylebone) give full details of the general holdings on these local theatres.

There are separate indexes to prints and photographs and to news cuttings.

LONDON

167 WESTMINSTER CITY LIBRARIES.
Westminster Archives and Local History Collection (Westminster Area)
Victoria Library, Buckingham Palace Road, London SW1W 9UD
(01) 798 2180

Contact	Archivist
Hours	Monday–Friday 9.30–7, Saturday 9.30–1, 2–5
Contents	The collection consists of programme, playbills, souvenirs, portraits, news and press cuttings, books and pamphlets, illustrations.

Programmes collection includes:

(a) covering London (approx. 80 boxes), the Provinces (4), Dublin (1), and Europe and U.S.A. (4). c.1860+

(b) 17 small bound volumes late 19th century — 1938 covering London, Paris, New York and Salzburg.

(c) 6 portfolios of programmes, playbills, cuttings and illustrations.

(d) 12 large scrapbooks 1830s–1939 programmes and review cuttings.

and Maschwitz, Eric *'London Theatres'.* Three volumes on London theatres and performances, using programmes, press cuttings and photographs.

Playbills for London and provinces, including Theatre Royal, Glasgow (5 vols.)

Newscuttings including 9 vols. relating to Her Majesty's Theatre 1844–1857

Adelphi Theatre: A license granted to Benjamin Webster 1844, and Mss return of takings 20 November–23 Deceber 1865

LONDON

168 WIMBLEDON SCHOOL OF ART. Library

Merton Hall Road, London SW19 3QA   (01) 540 0231

Contact	Librarian. Patricia Harrison
Admission	The Library is open to public for reference only on written application to the Librarian
Hours	Term time: Monday–Thursday 9–8.30, Friday 9–6 Vacations: Monday–Friday 9–1, 2–4.30
Contents	Book stock with particular emphasis on theatre design, both scenery and costume.
Catalogue	Internal — Card catalogue to book stock. Periodical articles indexed from 1979
Indexes	Published. Periodicals Bulletin (subject index). Irregular.

LOUGHBOROUGH

169 LOUGHBOROUGH UNIVERSITY OF TECHNOLOGY.
Pilkington Library

Loughborough, Leicestershire LE11 3TU   (0509) 63171

Telex	34319
Contact	Miss M. McKay
Admission	For reference, admission by application to the University Librarian
Hours	Term time: Monday–Friday 9–10, Saturday 9–5.30, Sunday 10–8 Vacations: Monday–Friday 9 5.30

| Contents | General collection to serve English and Drama Department. also: "19th century British drama: a collection of 780 plays", cf. CC Kohler Sales Catalogue 1982. |

LUTON
170   LUTON CENTRAL LIBRARY
St. George's Square, Luton   (0582) 30161

Telex	82347
Contact	R. P. Hawkes, ALA, District Librarian
Admission	Unrestricted
Hours	Monday–Friday 9–9, Saturday 9–5
Contents	George Bernard Shaw Collection containing 450 printed texts, 300 programmes and 400 press notices.

LUTON
171   LUTON MUSEUM AND ART GALLERY
Wardown Park, Luton, Bedfordshire   (0582) 36941

Contact	R. P. Hawkes, District Librarian
Hours	Daily 10.30–5
Contents	Small collection of material relating to Grand Theatre, Luton; and other local performances. Early 19th century playbills on London theatres:– Lyceum 1805 and 1808, Drury Lane 1801, Covent Garden 1812–26. Playbill for Theatre, Rochdale 1806.
Catalogue	Typed list available.

MAIDSTONE
172   KENT ARCHIVES OFFICE
County Hall, Maidstone, Kent ME14 1XH   (0622) 671411 Ext. 3312

Contact	W. Nigel Yates, County Archivist
Admission	Free to all serious enquirers
Hours	Monday–Friday 9–4.30 (under review)
Contents	Licensing records for Kent theatres in Quarter Sessions records (18th–19th centuries). References to payments to players in Faversham and New Romney (16th–17th centuries) borough collections. References to theatres, performances, actors in private collections — including several in *Sackville of Knole MSS* (ref U269). Sandwich Theatre playbills 1817–1848 in Sandwich borough collection. Manuscripts of *Comoedia Latina* by Abraham Faunce, *ante* 1586 in *De L'Isle MSS* (ref U1475 Z15); *Laurentius* by William Pitt, 1773 in *Stanhope MSS* (ref U1590 S5/C46–47).
Catalogue	Card index housed in Search Room.

MANCHESTER
173 MANCHESTER CENTRAL LIBRARY. Arts Library

St. Peter's Square, Manchester M2 5PD (061) 236 9422 Ext. 264

Telex	669475, 667149
Contact	Mrs Jeannett Canavan, Librarian, Arts Library
Admission	Unrestricted, but prior notice preferable
Hours	Monday–Friday 9–9, Saturday 9–5
Contents	The collection is restricted to theatres in the city of Manchester and contains approximately 25,000 playbills, 5,000 programmes. Press notices from 19th century onwards. Strong collections on Manchester Theatre Royal and Library Theatre, Manchester. Reasonable collections on most local theatres. Approximately 200 prints and photographs of interiors and exteriors of theatre buildings, plus periodical articles, newspaper cuttings and architectural plans.
Published guide	"The Manchester theatre; resources of the Arts Library" by Elizabeth Leach, FLA in *Manchester Review* Vol. 10 Autumn 1965. "Playbills and programmes" by Elizabeth Leach, FLA in *Manchester Review* Vol 11 Spring/Summer 1966.

MANCHESTER
174 MANCHESTER POLYTECHNIC. Capitol Library

School Lane, Didsbury, Manchester M20 10HT (061) 434 3331

Contact	Mrs Sachs
Admission	Application for external reader's tickets to Librarian.
Hours	Term time only: Monday–Thursday 10–4
Contents	The library serves the School of Theatre and concentrates on film, television and theatre monographs.

MANCHESTER
175 UNIVERSITY OF MANCHESTER. John Rylands University Library

Oxford Road, Manchester M13 9PP

Contact	C. J. Canner
Admission	Short term admission is freely available to persons pursuing serious research. Applications in writing to Head of Reader Services at least 3 days before admission is required.
Hours	Main Library: Term Time: Monday–Friday 9–9.30, Saturday 9–1 Vacations: Monday–Friday 9.30–5.30, Saturday 9.30–1 Deansgate Building: Monday–Friday 10–5.30, Saturday 10–1
Contents	Printed material to be expected in a major university library,

plus:

Main Library (Oxford Road)   (061) 273 3333 Ext. 3290
1) G. L. Brook Drama Collection. Play texts, works on drama and the theatre, c.300 programmes (mainly 1930s and 1940s). Author catalogue and subject catalogue.
2) Three Centuries of Drama: English 1500–1800; American 1714–1830. Published catalogue by G. W. Bergquist. Microprint cards in 28 boxes. Publisher: Readex Microprint

Deansgate Building (Deansgate, Manchester 3)
                                    (061) 834 5343
1) Miss A. E. F. Horniman material
   a) Two collections of extracts from periodicals 1903–1919 relating to the Abbey Theatre, Dublin, the Gaiety Theatre, Manchester, and the repertory movement in England. 10+16 vols.
   b) Letters from authors and playwrights relating to Miss Horniman's work in the theatre and their own work. c.100 items
2) Theatre Royal, Manchester. A collection of theatre playbills, concert programmes, etc. relating to the Theatre Royal, Manchester and other provincial and London theatres. 1808–72
3) Basil Dean Archive. Material relating to Dean's work in the theatre and cinema. More than 10,000 letters and papers, together with scrapbooks, scripts, prompt copies, 700+ programmes, photographs, designs.
4) Hugh Hunt Papers. Including files on plays, prompt copies of plays directed by Hunt, material relating to the Abbey Theatre, correspondence, programmes, press-cuttings, etc. c.1924–80
5) Stephen Joseph Papers. Relating to theatrical productions, c.1951–66, including the introduction of 'theatre in the round' at Scarborough and elsewhere. Designs, plans, photographs, writings by Joseph, correspondence, programmes, leaflets, etc.
6) A. N. Monkhouse Papers. General literary papers c.1898–1935, including correspondence relating to Monkhouse's plays and other plays
7) C. E. Montague Papers. General literary and journalistic papers, c.1880–1930. Including MSS. of Montague's plays and writings on drama; cuttings of his reviews for the Manchester Guardian and of reviews of his plays.
8) Allardyce Nicoll Collections. 19th century English plays (c.1000) Handlist.
9) Richard Cross, prompter to the theatres: Diary 1740–42 (Rylands English MS.1111): edited in *'Bulletin of the John Rylands Library'*, vol. 40.
10) Sarah and William Siddons: letters to Mrs H. L. Piozzi, 1793–

1807 (Rylands English MSS. 574 & 892) 27 items

MATLOCK

176 DERBYSHIRE RECORD OFFICE

County Offices, Matlock, Derbyshire DE4 3AG   (0629) 3411 Ext. 7347

Contact   Miss J. Sinar, County Archivist

Hours   Monday–Friday 9.30–1, 2–4.45 (it is essential to telephone in advance of a visit)

Contents   Handbills advertising Ashbourne Theatre 1818–44 (ref. D239 M/ F 10992–11004). Records of Licensing of theatres (18th and 19th centuries) in Derbyshire. Quarter Sessions Order Books. Miscellaneous material relating to Chesterfield Theatre, Corn Exchange Derby, Theatre Royal Derby, Tideswell Theatre and various individual performances. Memoirs, York Theatrical Co. at Doncaster, 19th century.

MIDDLESBOROUGH

177 MIDDLESBOROUGH CENTRAL LIBRARY

Victoria Square, Middlesborough, Cleveland   (0642) 248155

Telex   58439

Contact   F. Regan, County Librarian

Hours   Monday–Friday 9.30–7, Saturday 9.30–5

Contents   General library stock. Approximately 100 playbills and programmes 1860s on; also W. L. Pattinson Collection of material on local theatres and music halls for period c.1896–1959: includes 28 scrap books plus material on Theatre Royal Middlesborough, Castle Theatre Stockton, Empire Palace of Varieties Middlesborough and local concerts.

NEWCASTLE UPON TYNE

178 LAING ART GALLERY

Higham Place, Newcastle upon Tyne NE1 8AG   (0632) 327734

Contact   The Curator

Contents   Includes in its costume collection, a doublet worn by Sir Henry Irving.

NEWCASTLE UPON TYNE

179 NEWCASTLE CITY LIBRARIES. Local Studies Collection

Central Library, Princess Square, P.O. Box 1MC, Newcastle upon Tyne NE99 1MC   (0632) 610691

Contact   Local History Librarian

Hours   Monday–Thursday 9–9, Friday–Saturday 9–5

Contents	Extensive local collection of playbills and programmes. Reviews etc. covered in local papers, 1711 to date. Plans and licensing records of Theatre Royal, Newcastle. Printed histories of local theatres. Several thousand playbills in bound volumes. Press cuttings 1969–. Clark Programme Collection: 3,600 programmes — local, national and foreign 1876–1939. Holmes Programme Collection: 1,336 programmes — local, national and foreign 1860–1939

NEWCASTLE UPON TYNE

180 NORTHUMBERLAND RECORD OFFICE

Melton Park, North Gosforth, Newcastle upon Tyne NE3 5QX

(089426) 2680

Contact	R. M. Gard, County Archivist
Admission	Unrestricted
Hours	Tuesday–Thursday 9–5, Friday 9–4.30, Monday 9–9 (except Bank Holidays)
Contents	Title deeds of Old Theatre, Alnwich 1775–1920. A few licensing records relating to Newcastle and Alnwich. Act of Parliament & memoranda on Newcastle Theatre, plus notices 1824–30. Plans of Theatre Royal, Newcastle c.1897. Davison Collection of Theatre Bills, 1816–1851 for Alnwich and other Northumberland venues (c.240 playbills). Some 19th century playbills for Newcastle and Alnwich.
Indexes	Indexes of place, plays, actors, and companies in preparation.

NEWCASTLE UPON TYNE

181 TYNE AND WEAR COUNTY COUNCIL ARCHIVES DEPARTMENT

Blandford House, West Blandford Street, Newcastle upon Tyne NE1 4JA

(0632) 26789

Contact	County Archivist
Hours	Monday, Wednesday–Friday 8.45–5.15, Tuesday 8.45–8.30
Contents	Records of the Theatre Royal, Newcastle, 1785–1945, including 4 architects' plans, 14 licensing records, c.50 business records, c.100 financial records, c.35 letters. Deeds for the People's Theatre, Newcastle (formerly 18–22 Rye Hill), 1848–1860. Deeds etc. re Empire Theatre, Newcastle, 1894–1899, including valuation, articles of Association, sale agreement. Theatre programmes, Newcastle, Gateshead, London etc., c.1922– (c.20 items). Ledger of R. W. Younge, Tyne Theatre, 1886–1887 (Ref. 1123). Register of Theatre Licences, Gateshead Petty Session, 1923–1953 (Ref. 1290). Register of Theatre Licences, Hebburn Petty Sessions, 1912–1958 (Ref. 1292). Theatre and concert programmes for

Tyneside and Sunderland, 1895–1911 (Ref. 1433). Building plans (indexed) for Newcastle Theatres at Byker Bank, Percy Street (Haymarket and Palace), New Bridge Street, Northumberland Road (Olympia), Westgate Road (Tyne Theatre) and Shakespeare Street (Theatre Royal), 1876–1959 (Ref. T186). Building plans (indexed) for Newcastle Music Halls at Nelson Street, Shields Road, Grey Street (Old Oxford) and Croft Street, 1883–1894 (Ref. T186). Building plans (indexed) for Newcastle Picture Halls (Gem, Savoy and Gaitey), 1890 (Ref. T186). Theatre Royal, North Shields, playbills, 1853–1854. Whitley Bay Priory Theatre records, 1948–1974. Plan, Regal Theatre, Fenham, 1932. Also Robert Wood Collection relating to entertainment, formerly with the National Museum of Music Hall and the Fenwick Collection of circus ephemera.

NORTHAMPTON

182A NENE COLLEGE. Library

Moulton Park, Northampton NN2 2AL   (0604) 71500

Contact   M. Wilson

Admission   For reference

Hours   Term time: Monday–Friday 9–8
               Vacations: Monday–Friday 9–4

Contents   General collection of works on the theatre, and playtexts.

NORTHAMPTON

182B NORTHAMPTON MUSEUM AND ART GALLERY

Guildhall Road, Northampton NN1 1DR   (0604) 34881

Contact   Miss J. M. Swann, Keeper of the Boot and Shoe Collection

Hours   Monday–Saturday 10–6

Contents   Theatrical footwear.

Note   *Theatrephile*, Vol. 1, no. 3, June 1984. Theatrical footwear in Northampton Museum, by June Swann.

NORTHAMPTON

183 NORTHAMPTON RECORD OFFICE

Delapre Abbey, Northampton   (0604) 62129

Contact   P. King, Chief Archivist

Hours   Monday–Wednesday 9–4.45, Thursday 9–7.45, Friday 9–4.30, 1st & 3rd Saturday in month by appointment

Contents   Miscellaneous collection of playbills relating to local theatres, 18th–20th centuries. Northampton Theatre Syndicate Ltd. — Collection of business documents including inventories, minutes, share certificates, leases and agreements, bills, receipts, balance sheets, etc. for the years 1911–1959. Printed texts of *The Two Queens of Brentford* by the Duke of Buckingham, 1721; and the following by Fairfax L. Cartwright c.1890 — *Bianca Capello: a tragedy, The Emperor's Wish, Lorello, Graziella, The Baglioni: a tragedy,* plus associated press reviews, also manuscripts of texts by Fairfax L. Cartwright — *Her Majesty's Minister, The Faithful Shepherd: a pastoral, The Road to Oxford: a comedy* and manuscript of *Voyage to the Moon,* by a Gentleman, all mid 18th century. Playbill of amateur theatrical stage managed by Charles Dickens at Rockingham Castle, 1851. Daventry playbills: early 19th century. Knuston Hall playbill for private theatricals, c.1850. Licensing records for Northampton Theatre, 1932–41, and for Daventry (some letters). Correspondence of Creyke (playwright) and others, 1864–1872. Photographs of exterior and interior of New Theatre, Northampton (lighting and electrical plant), c.1910. Playbill of Kibworth (Leics.) Theatre for *'School for Scandal'* and *'Gretna Green',* 1802. Typescript text of Wootton Mummers play. Watford (Northants) Players record book 1926–1955. Business records of theatres used also as cinemas at Wellingborough and Rushden, 1910–31. File of letters of Jackman family, theatre owners and producers, 1846–1853. Two letters from Aaron Hill to the Duke of Montagu, 1722.

NORTHAMPTON

184 NORTHAMPTONSHIRE STUDIES COLLECTION

Central Library, Abington Street, Northampton NN1 2BA   (0604) 26774

Contact   Miss M. Arnold, Local History Librarian

Hours   Monday, Wednesday, Friday 9–5, Tuesday 9–5, Thursdays and Saturdays on application only.

Contents   Royal Theatre: programmes 1884–5, 1927+. New Theatre: programmes June 1952–1958, Sale of Contents 1959. Photographs of interior and exterior of New Theatre and Royal Theatre. Theatre, Marefair 1817–1848: c. 160 photocopies of playbills (originals in British Library). Playbills for theatres at Thrapston, Towcester, Peterborough, and Wellingborough. Richard Foulkes: *Northampton Repertory Theatre,* 1977. A. Perkins Dyas: *Adventure in Repertory,* 1948. Ernest Reynolds: *Northampton Repertory Theatre,* 1976. Lou Warwick: *Death of a theatre,* 1960; *Drama that smelled,* 1975; *The Mackenzies called Compton,* 1977; *Theatre unroyal,* 1974.

Indexes   Index to shows at the New Theatre 1952–6, 1957–8. Index to variety shows and artists at the New Theatre 1952–7. Index to articles in local periodicals.

NORWICH

185 NORFOLK RECORD OFFICE

Central Library, Norwich NR2 1NJ   (0603) 611277 Ext. 262

Contact	Jean Kennedy, County Archivist
Admission	It is advisable to contact the office in advance of visit
Hours	Monday–Friday 9–5, Saturday 9–12
Contents	The main collection of material of relevance to theatre historians is a series of documents relating to the Theatre Royal, Norwich, and theatres in Yarmouth and Colchester, administered jointly with the Theatre Royal in the early 19th century. The Norwich Company of Comedians has left a record of its circuit in the late 18th century and early 19th century, which gives details of places, dates and plays performed.

Theatre Royal, Norwich, built 1757: Building leases, agreement about wardrobes and properties, employment contracts, and 18th century Lord Chamberlain's licence. Theatre Committee minutes, 1768–1858. Norwich, Yarmouth and Colchester theatres' receipts and accounts. Copy playbills, 1800–1820. Norwich, Yarmouth and King's Lynn press cuttings for 19th and 20th centuries. Some 19th century correspondence. Norwich Theatre wardrobe and properties list for 1858. Maddermarket and Theatre Royal: 18 programmes 1814–1923. Theatre Royal, Norwich: Records containing contracts, correspondence, wage records, etc. for 1950s and 1960s.

Other theatre records are scattered through miscellaneous collections and are indexed by the names of places or individual actors and dramatists, including:

MS of *The Green Man*, a play c.1816. Copy of Act II of *The Carnival of Venice*. MS Notes on Norwich Theatres 1826–50. Yarmouth and Norwich petty sessions records contain 20th century licences. Papers of Nugent B. Monck and records of the Norwich Players and the Maddermarket Theatre Trust, c.1900–1978, including plays by Monck, 1906–1955; programmes, cast lists, newspaper cuttings, etc. relating to Monck's productions; minute books and the administrative records of the Norwich Players; designs for settings and backcloths; programmes, posters, cuttings, etc. relating to Maddermarket productions. MS of *The Grange*, a comedy (?by the Rev. Jermyn Pratt) 18th century. MS of *Ragandjaw*, by David Garrick, with letters and poem by Garrick, c.1760s. MS of *The Odd Whim* or *Two at a Time* by Humfrey Repton, a comedy in five acts' c.1780; illustrated with designs for sets. Martham playbills, 1804, 1836, 1842. Assignments of shares in Yarmouth Theatre, 1799, 1804–1876. Records of granting of theatre licences in Norwich and Yarmouth Quarter Sessions books, c.18th–19th centuries. King's Lynn borough records (can be consulted at Lynn or at Norwich: two weeks' advance notice advisable): grants of theatre licences in Borough Sessions records, c.18–19th centuries; New Theatre committee minutes 1813–1840; inventory and bill for scenery at New Theatre, 1815.

NORWICH

186 UNIVERSITY OF EAST ANGLIA. Library

Norwich NR4 7TJ   (0603) 56161

Contact	John Kimber, Librarian
Admission	On application to the Librarian
Hours	Term time: Monday–Thursday 9–10, Friday 9–8
	Vacations: Monday–Friday 9–6
Contents	In addition to the standard materials to be found in a university library, there is:

The Holloway Collection of Modern Culture Records:
apart from some scrap books, containing reviews and programmes of plays, mainly in East Anglia, the collection consists of ephemeral material, a wide range of institutions, art centres, local theatres etc. covering cultural and artistic events throughout the U.K. since the 1970s.

Guide   A leaflet describing the collection is available.

NOTTINGHAM

187 NOTTINGHAMSHIRE COUNTY LIBRARY

Local Studies Library, Angel Row, Nottingham NG1 6HP

(0602) 412121 Ext. 48

Contact	Sheila M. Cooke, Local Studies Librarian
Hours	Monday–Friday 9.30–8, Saturday 9–1
Contents	Scripts etc: about 400 scripts on deposit from The Playhouse — a card index by title of production. Playbills and programmes: several thousand, c.1780 onward — card index by title 1780–1867, 1900 to date. Photographs: c.1,000 both on deposit from the Playhouse and Library's own collection. Many scrapbooks and press cuttings. 5 tape recordings of interviews. Nottingham Theatres covered by the collection include Theatre, St. Mary's Gate, Theatre Royal, Playhouse (old and new) and the Empire.

NOTTINGHAM

188 NOTTINGHAM RECORD OFFICE

County House, High Pavement, Nottingham NG1 1HR   (0602) 504524

Contact	A. J. M. Henstock, Principal Archivist
Hours	Daily 9–4.45, except Tuesday 9–7.15, Saturday 9–12.15. Material

produced hourly.

Contents   5 playbills, 1 architect's account, 5 licensing records, 5 deeds. Theatre Royal (Nottingham) scrapbook, Grand Theatre (Nottingham) scrapbook.

NOTTINGHAM
189 UNIVERSITY OF NOTTINGHAM LIBRARY

University Park, Nottingham NG7 2RD   (0602) 506161 Ext. 3433

Telex   37346

Contact   Michael Brook, Special Collections Librarian

Hours   Monday–Friday 9–5

Contents   Cambridge Drama Collection:
consisting of English plays published between 1750 and 1850, together with works on the English theatre, (but not drama as a literary form) during the same period, was presented to the University in 1960 by the Cambridge City Libraries, to which much of it had been given by Henry Thomas Hall during the 1870s and 1880s. A number of volumes had belonged to the Cambridge Garrick Club. The collection consists of over 300 volumes, a number of which are bound volumes of pamphlets, there being over 1,200 individual plays in all.
Catalogue:
All the plays have author entries in the main catalogue as well as in a separate catalogue kept on the Dept. of Special Collections, which also contains analytical entries for plays of the period forming part of anthologies or collected works.
Cambridge Shakespeare Collection:
The 'Shakespeare Memorial Library' of Cambridge City Libraries was presented to the University at the same time as the Drama Collection. It originally consisted of works by Shakespeare and books about his life and art. The books on Shakespeare have been added to the University Library's general stock, so that the Cambridge Shakespeare Collection now consists almost exclusively of about 250 editions of Shakespeare's plays including separate plays and poems.
Woodward Collection of Parker Woodward (1854–1931):
was presented to the University in 1945. It consists of over 300 titles on the Bacon-Shakespeare controversy.

NOTTINGHAM
190 UNIVERSITY OF NOTTINGHAM LIBRARY.
Manuscripts Department

University Park, Nottingham   (0602) 50601 Ext. 3440

Contact   A. Cameron, Keeper of the Manuscripts

Admission   To bona fide researchers

Contents	The Manuscript Department is a general repository containing many collections of MSS, from12th to 20th century, relating to manorial, estate, personal, business, official, literary, etc. One 'collection' may contain many of these categories of records. The majority of the items relative to theatre research occur in the Portland Collection (belonging to the Trustees of the 7th Duke of Portland and deposited in the University) both in the literary section and among the personal papers of the family. Others are in the Marlay Collection of personal papers, mainly social/literary. Handlists of the collections are available within the Manuscript Department and at the Historical Manuscript Commission (National Register of Archives) in London, and in the copyright libraries. The early part of the Marlay letters has been edited and published by R. Warwick Bond, *The Marlay Letters,* 1778–1820.

Portland Collection includes 11 volumes containing 17th century plays, including some of Shadwell and the Duke of Newcastle. There is also: 1 paper listing names of subscribers to building new theatre in the Haymarket, early 18th century. 7 papers relating to the opera, early 18th century. 1 letter each from Thomas Shadwell and D. Garrick.

Marlay Collection includes letters from Mrs Fanny Abington, a note from R. B. Sheridan, 2 letters from Mrs Siddons, one from her daughter re. her death and one letter from Talma.

Other miscellaneous items including references to the above persons in the letters of Lady Charleville, Mrs Opie and Maria Edgeworth.

OXFORD

191   BODLEIAN LIBRARY

Oxford OX1 3BG		(0865) 44675
Telex	83656	
Contact	The Keeper of Printed Books	
Admission	Bona fide researchers	
Hours	Monday–Friday 9–10 (University term), 9–7 (Vacation)	
Contents	The Bodleian Library is one of the Copyright Deposit Libraries in the United Kingdom and as such is a major research centre.	

The John Johnson Collection of Printed Ephemera:
covers all types of material; the theatre section consists of between 250 and 300 boxes, but is growing all the time. It chiefly comprises programmes and playbills, but also includes other material. There is no catalogue, but partial indexes of playbills, actors and actresses are available. cf. Jennifer Tonkin's note in *Theatre Notebook,* Winter 1971/2.

OXFORD

192 OXFORDSHIRE COUNTY LIBRARIES. Local History Collections

Central Library, Westgate, Oxford OX1 1DJ   (0865) 815749

Contact   Malcolm Graham

Hours   Monday, Tuesday, Wednesday, Friday 9.15–7, Thursday and
               Saturday 9.15–5

Contents   Printed books, articles and cuttings on local theatres. Oxford
               theatre programmes, 1882+ (very incomplete). Photographs,
               cuttings and programmes relating to Oxford Dramatic Societies,
               c.1946+. Posters of local theatres and dramatic performances,
               c.1970+. Files of local newspapers and magazines advertising and
               reviewing plays and shows.

Indexes   Jackson's Oxford Journal synopsis and index 1753–1790. Oxford
               Mail and Times index 1971–1984.

OXFORD

193 OXFORDSHIRE COUNTY RECORD OFFICE

County Hall, Oxford OX1 1ND   (0865) 815203

Contact   Any member of Archive Department

Hours   Monday–Thursday 9–1, 2–5, Friday 9–1, 1–4

Contents   Little material on Oxfordshire theatres. Birmingham Gaiety
               Theatre of Varieties 1899–1912: share certificates.

OXFORD

194 WORCESTER COLLEGE

Oxford   (0865) 47251

Contact   Miss L. Montgomery, Librarian

Admission   Bona fide researchers by arrangement (Monday–Friday), but not
               after 6.00 pm

Contents   6 MSS plays, 20 playbills, 6 paintings and drawings by Inigo Jones
               and John Webb. Collection of 5,000 plays of 16th–18th
               centuries.

PLYMOUTH

195 CITY OF PLYMOUTH MUSEUM AND ART GALLERY

Drake Circus, Plymouth PL4 8AJ   (0752) 668000 Ext. 4372

Contact   Miss M. V. Attrill, Keeper of Art

Hours   Monday–Friday 10–6. Saturday 10–5

Contents   300–400 playbills dating from 19th century, and relating to the
               theatres of Plymouth, particularly the Theatre Royal. A number of
               photographs, drawings and paintings of Plymouth theatre

exteriors. Also Cottonian Collection includes a number of volumes of plays including some first editions of John Gay.

PLYMOUTH

196   PLYMOUTH CENTRAL LIBRARY

Drake Circus, Plymouth, Devon PL4 8AL   (0752) 21312 Ext. 4680

Telex	45578 WESTLIB G
Contact	Music and Drama or Local History Library
Hours	Music and Drama Library: Monday–Thursday 9.30–6.30, Friday 9.30–8, Saturday 9.30–4
	Local History Library: Monday–Friday 9–9, Saturday 9–4
Contents	Music and Drama Library has a collection of scrapbooks of programmes and criticism covering amateur and professional theatre in South Devon. There are approximately 2,400 programmes and reviews.
	Local History Department contains playbills for Palace Theatre, 1948–56, plus programmes for the Grand, 1889–97, St. James Hall, 1871, Theatre Royal, 1802–1932, and Plymouth Circus, 1847–52. There are also theatre scrapbooks for 1821–26.

POOLE

197   POOLE ARCHIVES COLLECTION

Municipal Buildings, Civic Centre, Poole, Dorset BH15 2RU   (0202) 675151

Contact	Town Clerk's Department
Contents	Includes petitions for theatre licences and petition for banning of theatre by Poole people. 1790–1835. 25 documents. (Quarter Sessions Theatre 1–25)

POOLE

198   POOLE GUILDHALL MUSEUM

Market Street, Poole, Dorset BH15 1NP   (0202) 675151

Contact	Curator
Hours	Monday–Saturday 10–5, Sunday 2–5
Contents	A few programmes and playbills.

POOLE

199   POOLE REFERENCE LIBRARY

Arndale Centre, Poole, Dorset BH15 1QE   (0202) 671496

Contact	Reference Librarian
Hours	Monday–Friday 9.30–7, Saturday 9–1
Contents	Selection of material relating to current local arts centre.

PRESTON
200 LANCASHIRE COUNTY MUSEUM SERVICE
Stanley Street, Preston, Lancashire PR1 4YP   (0772) 264061

Contact	County Museum Officer
Admission	By appointment only
Contents	Programmes, posters, photographs and postcards relating to Blackpool theatres c.1940s+
Note	Duplicated list of holdings available.

PRESTON
201 LANCASHIRE RECORD OFFICE
Bow Lane, Preston, Lancashire PR1 8ND   (0772) 58347

Contact	K. Hall, County Archivist
Hours	Tuesday 9–8.30, Wednesday–Friday 9–5, closed Mondays
Contents	17th century material includes letter referring to a Royal Masque 7th February 1608; information on a performance of Henry VIII 1632; will of William Sandes of Preston bequeathing 'my shewe called the Chaos' 1638; statement by William Newsham on people who have acted plays and interludes 1647/8.

18th century material on Preston Theatre, including letter describing Garrick performance.

19th century material includes programmes and playbills for a number of Lancashire theatres and some London theatres, plus:

Preston Theatre Royal; correspondence, playbills, accounts and deeds 1867–1879. Theatre Royal, Oldham; daily returns 1884–5. Colosseum Theatre; account book 1901–3. Empire Theatre, Oldham; ledger 1899–1913. Grant Theatre, Oldham; account book 1913–1917. Puppet theatre scenery (c.1850)

20th century material includes file of correspondence relating to Palace Theatre, Barrow, 1920–1930.

RAMSGATE
202 RAMSGATE MUSEUM
Ramsgate Library, Guildford Lawn, Ramsgate   (0843) 53532

Contacts	M. Winsch, Curator Miss I. Huckstep, Librarian
Hours	Library hours: Monday & Friday 9.30–8, Tuesday & Thursday 9.30–7, Saturday 9.30–1
Contents	2 programmes for Palace Theatre c.1900, Programme for Sangers Amphitheatre, c.1900.

READING

203 BULMERSHE COLLEGE OF HIGHER EDUCATION. Library

Woodlands Avenue, Earley, Reading RG6 1HY   (0734) 663387 Ext. 232

Contact	Barbara Morris
Admission	For reference
Hours	Term time: Monday–Friday 9–9, Saturday 9.30–12.30
	Vacations: Monday–Friday 9–5
Contents	General published material on theatre and drama (approximately 2,000 vols.)

READING

204 BERKSHIRE RECORD OFFICE

Shire Hall, Reading RG1 3EY   (0734) 875444 Ext. 3182

Contact	J. A. S. Green, County Archivist
Admission	Unrestricted; no documents are produced between 12.45–2 or less than 30 minutes before closing. For readers arriving after 5 pm advance booking is advisable.
Hours	Monday 2–5, Tuesday & Wednesday 9–5, Thursday 9–9, Friday 9–4.30
Contents	Quarter Sessions records from 1703, with separate commissions in 7 boroughs, include registration of theatres.

Material relating to actors:

1517–88: Payments by Abingdon borough to named companies of players, including the Queen's players, the Earl of Leicester's and many others (A/FAc 1,2)

20th century: Notes by A. E. Preston on visits of companies to Abingdon, from the records above (D/EP 7/83)

c.1670: Suit in Abingdon Borough Court for breach of covenant between an acrobat and the manager of troupe (D/EP 7/136)

1621–2: Payments to 'kings and queens and prince's players' by the Borough of Wallingford (W/FAb 3)

1599: Payment to the Queen's players in Wallingford Borough accounts (W/FAb 1)

Material relating to theatres:

1803: Deeds of shares in Drury Lane and Co. Gdn. (L/EBp T140/11)

1776: Assignment by D. Garrick of properties near Drury Lane Theatre, referring to George III's grant to him to perform plays in the theatre (D/EEg T1)

Items on charitable collections in Berkshire for relief of suffering caused by London theatre fires 1672 and 73; and assignment of silver tickets for Opera House, Haymarket and list of creditors, including performers at the King's Theatre (D/EHe T1)

1742–1744: Letter on the possibility of a fire proof safety curtain for a Playhouse (DEHy B4/1)

1788–1798: Notebook containing list of plays, operas and entertainments at London theatres (D/EBt B25)

Published guides	Lists are being published by Chadwyck-Healey as part of their series on British Archives.

READING

205 BRITISH BROADCASTING CORPORATION.

Written Archives Centre

Caversham Park, Reading, Berkshire RG4   (0734) 472742 Ext. 280

Contact	Mrs J. M. Kavanagh, Written Archives Officer
Admission	Open, by prior appointment only, to researchers engaged on a serious project. Enquiries can be dealt with by correspondence. Charges made for certain services.
	The purpose of the collection is to make available, subject to certain restrictions of which copyright is the most important, documents, files and press cuttings relating to the full range of the BBC's activities from 1922 to 1962.
Hours	Tuesday–Friday 9.45–5.15
Contents	A deposit collection of all BBC publications including *The Listener* and *Radio Times*. Approximately 12 feet of MSS radio plays. (The remainder are held by Radio Drama Play Library in Broadcasting House. TV plays are held by T.V. Drama Script Unit at Television Centre.) The catalogues of both libraries have been published on microfiche. Approximately 1 foot of papers relating to the BBC Repertory Company. Approximately 150 feet of press cuttings on broadcasting.
	Large numbers of programme files, Radio and TV, including outside broadcasts from theatres, as well as studio productions.
	Large collections of correspondence between theatrical figures and BBC about their contributions to programmes, as well as scripts of talks and discussions.

READING

206 READING UNIVERSITY LIBRARY

P.O. Box 223, Whiteknights, Reading RG6 2AE   (0734) 874331 Ext. 134

Contact	Michael Bott, Keeper of Archives and Manuscripts
Admission	By appointment
Hours	Tuesday–Friday 9–1, 2–5
Contents	Samuel Beckett Collection:
	Manuscripts and typescripts of plays,
	Notebooks relating to various productions directed by Beckett,

Copies of published plays annotated by Beckett,
Posters, programmes, photographs and other publicity material
for numerous productions in the United Kingdom and abroad
of Beckett's plays.

Catalogue   *The Samuel Beckett Collection: a catalogue.* 1978. £2.50, with three
free supplements.

REDRUTH

207   CORNWALL COUNTY LIBRARY. Local Studies Library

2-4 Clinton Road, Redruth, Cornwall TR15 2QE   (0209) 216760

Contact   Librarian

Hours   Tuesday–Thursday 9.30–5, Friday 9.30–7, Saturday 9.30–12.30.
Closed for lunch 12.30–1.30 daily

Contents   Small, but growing, collection of programmes: Cornish stage
productions, mainly amateur 1945+. Collection of local posters
advertising theatrical events in Cornwall 1976+.

RICHMOND, Surrey

208   RICHMOND CENTRAL REFERENCE LIBRARY

Central Library, Little Green, Richmond TW9 1QL   (01) 940 5529

Note   (From the end of 1986 the collection will move to The Old Town
Hall, Whittaker Avenue. There will be an alteration in opening
hours.)

Contact   Local Studies Collection

Admission   Preferably by appointment

Hours   Monday, Thursday, Friday 10–6; Tuesday, Saturday 10–5,
Wednesday 10–8

Contents   Extensive collection of playbills, cuttings, prints, photographs and
documents on the Theatre Royal, Richmond.

Press cuttings, programmes, posters and photographs of
productions at the present Richmond Theatre (particularly
1950+). Some items on the Barnes Theatre, and other local
theatres.

Sladen Collection includes letters from early 20th century theatre
personalities, playwrights etc. but mainly of a social nature.

Indexes   Chronological list of Theatre Royal playbills; this collection is
currently being indexed fully by Dr Kathleen Barker.
Chronological index to Richmond Theatre material is in
preparation. Sladen Collection has a summary index.

RICHMOND

see also
LONDON. Public Record Office
Ruskin Avenue, Kew, Richmond, Surrey

ROCHDALE

209 ROCHDALE LOCAL STUDIES LIBRARY

The Esplanade, Rochdale OL16 1AQ   (0706) 47474 Ext. 423

Contact   Local Studies Librarian

Hours   Monday, Tuesday, Thursday 9.30–7.30, Wednesday 9.30–5, Friday 9.30–5.30, Saturday 9.30–4

Contents   Theatre posters 1794–1880: several hundred

Note   The majority of the posters are undergoing conservation processes. They are thus not available for consultation at the present time.

ROYSTON

210 ROYSTON AND DISTRICT MUSEUM

Lower King Street, Royston SG8 7DA   (0763) 42587

Contact   The Curator

Hours   Wednesday–Saturday 10–5, or by appointment

Contents   Material related to local amateur drama and musical societies dating back to 1830s. It includes programmes, photographs, theatre licensing applications and some handwritten prologues and altered texts.

RUTHIN

211 CLWYD RECORD OFFICE

46 Clwyd Street, Ruthin LL15 1HP   (08242) 3077

Contact   A. G. Veysey, County Archivist

Hours   Monday–Thursday 9–4.45, Friday 9–4.15

Contents   Playbills relating to Wolves Head Theatre, Denbigh; Theatre Royal, Wrexham; Latimer's Mammoth Theatre.

SALFORD

212 SALFORD LOCAL HISTORY LIBRARY

Peel Park, Salford M5 4WU   (061) 736 3353

Contact   Tim Ashworth

Hours   Monday, Wednesday, Thursday 9–5, Tuesday, Friday 9–7, Saturday 9–1

Contents   Newspaper cuttings, programmes, photographs relating to Salford Theatres.

Indexes   Included in General Information Catalogue.

SCARBOROUGH

213 NORTH YORKSHIRE COUNTY LIBRARY

Vernon Road, Scarborough, North Yorkshire YO11 2NN   (0723) 364285

Contact	B. Berryman
Hours	Monday–Thursday 10–5.30, Friday 10–7, Saturday 10–4
Contents	Scarborough Theatre c.1800–1836: approx 300 handbills. Londes-borough Theatre, Scarborough 1877–1891: 3 bound volumes of programmes. Opera House, Scarborough 1947–9: Publicity Manager's reports. Stephen Joseph Theatre in the Round: newspaper cuttings file. Also miscellaneous programmes, display bills etc. for some other local theatres.
Indexes	Index to local newspapers.

SHEFFIELD

214 SHEFFIELD CENTRAL LIBRARY

Surrey Street, Sheffield S1 1XZ   (0742) 734753

Contact	J. M. Olive, Local History Librarian
Hours	Monday–Friday 9–5.30, Saturday 9–4.30
Contents	Collection of material on Sheffield Playhouse, 1925–70. Wilkinson Collection: approximately 1,000 early 19th century playbills (chronological list only available); includes various theatres, halls etc. Crucible Theatre; programmes and publicity material since 1971 (Owing to deteriorating condition of paper, part of this collection cannot be made available until conservation completed.) Miscellaneous programmes of other Sheffield theatres.

SHEFFIELD

215 SHEFFIELD CITY MUSEUM

Weston Park, Sheffield S10 2TP   (0742) 27226

Contact	D. Bostwick
Hours	Daily 10–5
Contents	25 posters relating to Sheffield theatres and music hall, plus some theatre programmes. Earliest poster 1790.

SHREWSBURY

216 SHROPSHIRE LOCAL STUDIES LIBRARY

Castle Gates, Shrewsbury SY1 2AS   (0743) 61058

Contact	Local Studies Librarian
Hours	Monday, Wednesday 9.30–5.30, Tuesday, Friday 9.30–7.30, Saturday 9.30–5; closed daily 12.30–1.30 and all day Thursday

Contents	41 playbills relating to the Theatre (later Theatre Royal); 1 each for Royal County Theatre, Theatre, Bridge Place, Hills Lane House and Latimer's Theatre. Playbills also for Theatres at Ludlow, Pradoe and Newport. Additional material still remains to be sorted.

SHREWSBURY

217 SHROPSHIRE RECORD OFFICE

Shirehall, Abbey Foregate, Shrewsbury   (0743) 222407

Contact	County Archivist
Hours	Monday & Thursday 9–5, Friday 9–4, closed Tuesdays & Wednesdays
Contents	Several hundred playbills for shows (plays, scenes, dramatic recitals and various entertainments) in Shrewsbury, late 18th–19th centuries.

SIDCUP

218 ROSE BRUFORD COLLEGE. Library

Lamorbey Park, Sidcup, Kent DA15 9DF   (01) 300 3024

Contact	Christopher Edwards
Admission	For reference use by prior arrangement. Most material available through inter-library loan.
Hours	Term time: Monday, Wednesday, Friday 9–6, Tuesday & Thursday 9–8. Vacations: Monday–Friday 9.30–5
Contents	General college library (20,000+ volumes) with strong emphasis on theatre/drama. 500 play sets. 19,000 colour slides of set designs/theatre history.
Catalogue	Internal — GEAC on-line catalogue.

SMALLHYTHE

219 ELLEN TERRY MEMORIAL MUSEUM

Smallhythe Place, Smallhythe, Tenterden, Kent TN30 7NG
                                                        (05806) 2334/3134

Contact	Mrs M. Weare, Custodian in Charge
Hours	Daily, except Tuesday and Friday, from April–October 2–6 (appointment required)
Contents	Ellen Terry's working scripts, which can be studied on written application. Portraits, drawings, prints etc. are displayed, as are a number of the best costumes worn by Ellen Terry. In addition there are also costumes of Irving, Fred Terry and of William Terriss. A large number of exhibits relate to the Terry-Irving partnership and theatrical designs of Edward Gordon Craig. Other items include diaries, letters, momentos, costume drawings

etc. The house was the country home of Ellen Terry from 1899 until her death in 1928.

Catalogue   Available, £2.25 including postage.

SOUTH SHIELDS

220   SOUTH TYNESIDE CENTRAL LIBRARY

Prince Georg Street, South Shields, Tyne and Wear NE33 2PP (0632) 568841

Contact   Miss D. Johnson, Local History Librarian

Hours   Monday–Thursday 10–7, Friday 10–5, Saturday 10–12, 1–4. At least 24 hours notice of intended visit would be appreciated; more flexible hours could possibly be arranged.

Contents   c.50 playbills relating to South Shields Theatres. c.200 photographs of theatrical personalities. Newspaper cuttings on South Shields Theatres; books on local theatres. Photographs of local theatres.

Indexes   To newscuttings and theatre photographs.

SOUTHAMPTON

221   SOUTHAMPTON CITY RECORD OFFICE

Civic Centre, Southampton SO9 4XR   (0703) 223855 Ext. 2251

Contact   City Archivist

Hours   Monday–Friday 9–1, 1.30–5

Contents   Theatre programmes, mainly 20th century, scattered throughout the Miscellaneous Small Deposits Collection (Ref D/Z followed by the number of the deposit). This collection is not subject indexed. One or two of these small deposits have c.50–100 programmes, and several more have c.20–50.

STAFFORD

222   STAFFORDSHIRE COUNTY RECORD OFFICE

County Buildings, Eastgate Street, Stafford   (0785) 3121 Ext. 7910

Contact   F. B. Stitt, County Librarian and Archivist

Hours   Monday–Thursday 9–1, 2–5, Friday 9–1, 2–4.30

Contents   Deeds, including abstract of title to ¼ of Covent Garden Theatre, 1773 (D. 1788, P6, B12). Theatre, Lichfield: Lease and mortgage 1798, 1881 and 1890 (D.1851/8/54 and 56). Minutes of Macclesfield Theatre 1837–1869 (D877/204). Also includes: Stourbridge, release of 1856; licence from Master of Revels to Gabriel Fisher to act plays etc. 1714; Privy Seal licences to establish various theatres, 1756–93; Corn Exchange, Wolverhampton, licences, 1891–7; letters from Henry Irving, 1888.

STAFFORD

223 WILLIAM SALT LIBRARY

19 Eastgate Street, Stafford (0785) 52276

Contact   F. B. Stitt, County Archivist and William Salt Librarian

Hours   Tuesday–Thursday 9.30–12.45, 1.45–5, Friday 9.30–12.45, 1.45–
            4.30, Saturday 9.30–1

Contents   Approximately 280 playbills. Papers of Richard Brinsley Sheridan,
            including correspondence, agreements, speech by Mrs Siddons at
            last appearance, part of a manuscript tragedy, and an account book.
            Mainly c.1790–1812 (SMS 343).

STANLEY

224 BEAMISH NORTH OF ENGLAND OPEN AIR MUSEUM

Beamish Hall, Stanley, County Durham DH9 0RG (0207) 231811

Contact   Museum Director

Admission   Researchers by appointment

Hours   Easter–Mid September: Daily 10–6 (last admission 4)
            Mid September–Easter: Daily 10–5 (last admission 3).
            Closed Monday

Contents   Collection of miscellaneous theatre posters relating to the North
            East of England.

Indexes   Internal indexes to museum collections.

STOCKPORT

225 STOCKPORT CENTRAL LIBRARY

Wellington Road South, Stockport SK1 3RS (061480) 2966/3038/7297

Contact   T. D. W. Reid, Reference Librarian, Local Studies

Hours   Lending Library: Monday, Tuesday, Friday 9–8, Wednesday 9–5,
            Saturday 9–12 noon
            Reference Library: Monday–Friday 9–8, Saturday 9–12 noon

Contents   Local material: 70 playbills for Stockport Theatre. 1823–26;
            programmes issued by the Stockport Garrick Society for their
            productions at their Garrick Theatre; programmes of
            Hippodrome Theatre, Stockport, 1940–50. *The Theatre in Stockport*,
            by William Brackenbury, 1974 (Typescript). *Theatre Royal, Stockport
            1888–1938*, 1938. *Memories of the Theatre Royal*: articles in *The
            Advertiser*, 1958.

STRATFORD UPON AVON

226A ROYAL SHAKESPEARE GALLERY

Stratford upon Avon, Warwickshire   (0789) 296655

Contact   Brian Glover, Director

Contents   Paintings, costumes and other items relating to Shakespeare, productions of his plays and actors who have appeared in them.

STRATFORD UPON AVON

226B SHAKESPEARE CENTRE LIBRARY

Henley Street, Stratford upon Avon CV37 6QW   (0789) 4016

Contact   Dr Levi Fox, Director

Hours   Monday–Friday 10–5, Saturday 9.30–12.30

The Shakespeare Birthplace Trust Library, founded 1862, and Shakespeare Memorial Theatre Library, founded 1880, amalgamated to form the Shakespeare Centre Library in 1964. It exists as a research library for the life, work and times of William Shakespeare, incorporating the Royal Shakespeare Theatre collection.

Contents   The library contains approximately 35,000 volumes, including some 1,050 prompt copies. Printed play texts cover drama from Shakespeare's quartos to the present day, and are particularly strong on editions of Shakespeare from 1623. Approximately 5,700 playbills and programmes. Recordings of productions include c.60 sound recordings, 10 films, 5,600 production photographs (1920 onwards), 800 slides and 5,000 prints and illustrations. A few photographs of rehearsals. Costume designs for Shakespeare Memorial Theatre/RST productions from 1919. Set designs and other production records for approximately 100 productions at RST and Aldwych. Reviews and press notices for SMT/RSC productions 1879 onwards. Plans, business records etc. relating to SMT/RSC. Approximately 1,000 volumes of biography. Small collection of 19th century autographs. Picture collection totalling c.5,000 items. Some recorded interviews. Collections include archives of the Shakespeare Memorial Theatre (1879–1926 and 1932–60) and for the Royal Shakespeare Company in Stratford, London and on tour, 1960 onwards. Special collection — Bram Stoker Collection of material relating to Henry Irving and the Lyceum Theatre, c.2,000 items.

SUNDERLAND

227 SUNDERLAND MUSEUM AND ART GALLERY

Borough Road, Sunderland, Tyne and Wear SR1 1RP   (0783) 41235

Contact   Rosemary Crook, or Neil Sinclair

Hours	Monday–Friday 10–5.30, Saturday 10–4.30, Sunday 2–5
Contents	Plans of Sunderland 'Light' Theatre 1800–1900. Playbills and posters. Collection is almost exclusively of Sunderland, also includes Drury Lane, Lyceum, Empire, Kings and Royalty.

SUTTON

228 SUTTON CENTRAL LIBRARY

St. Nicholas Way, Sutton, Surrey   (01) 661 5050

Hours	Tuesday–Friday 9.30–8, Saturday 9.30–5
Contents	Small amount of local theatre material.

SWINDON

229 SWINDON DIVISIONAL LIBRARARY. Local Studies Library

Regent Circus, Swindon SN1 1QG   (0793) 27211

Contact	Reference Librarian
Hours	Monday–Friday 8.30–5.30
Contents	Small collection relating to the Queens Theatre (Empire Theatre) and the Playhouse, and the Wyvern Theatre and Arts Centre, all in Swindon.

TAUNTON

230 SOMERSET RECORD OFFICE

Obridge Road, Taunton, Somerset TA2 7PU   (0823) 87600

Contact	D. M. M. Shorrocks, County Archivist
Admission	Unrestricted
Hours	Monday–Thursday 9–4.50, Friday 9–4.20, Saturday by appointment
Contents	Playbills, 3 vols. relating to 1799–1833 for Taunton Theatre. 41 loose bills 1843–1857 for Chard Theatre. Licensing records: Occasional entries in the Order Books of the court of Quarter Sessions for the County. Small collection relating to Sir Henry Irving, partly given by Mrs Gabrielle Enthoven, including programmes (1872–1903), photographs and ephemera (DD/SAS C/2401/16). Playbills (1 vol) 1813–20 for Crewkerne Theatre. Also many individual items on national and Somerset theatres.
Note	The collection of original watercolours, drawings and prints of English theatres and scenery, possibly the working papers of Benjamin Wyatt, a theatrical architect, which was listed in the first edition has since been sold for the depositors by Lawrences of Crewkerne.

TAUNTON

231 TAUNTON LOCAL HISTORY LIBRARY

The Castle, Castle Green, Taunton TA1 4AD

Contact	David Bromwich, Librarian
Hours	Tuesday–Friday 9.30–12.30, 2–5.30, Saturday 9.30–12.30, 2–4
Contents	3 manuscript and 20 published texts of plays by local authors, including some in dialect. Approximately 70 printed biographies and biographical articles on Sir Henry Irving, a native of Somerset.

TORQUAY

232 TORQUAY CENTRAL LIBRARY

Lymington Road, Torquay TQ1 3DT   (0803) 217673

Hours	Monday–Wednesday, Friday 9–7, Thursday 9–6, Saturday 9–4
Contents	Pavilion Theatre Torquay: Virtually complete set of programmes for 1936–1954. A miscellaneous small collection for professional and amateur performances at Torbay venues from 1954+.

TOTNES

233 DARTINGTON COLLEGE OF ARTS. Library and Resources Centre

Totnes, Devon TQ9 6EJ   (0803) 862224

Contact	Dorothy Faulkner
Admission	Public given access for reference use. External borrower status on application.
Hours	Term time: Monday–Friday 9–9, Saturday & Sunday 1.30–5.30 Vacations: Monday–Friday 9–5
Contents	General stock includes approximately 1,500 books on theatre and dance to meet needs of students.

TROWBRIDGE

234 WILTSHIRE COUNTY RECORD OFFICE

County Hall, Trowbridge, Wiltshire BA14 8JG   (02214) 3641 Ext. 3502

Contact	County Archivist
Hours	Monday–Friday 9–5, late opening Wednesday to 8.30. No documents produced 12.30–1.30 and after 4.30 except Wednesday
Contents	5 playbills covering 1776–1812 (Wilts. RO 9, Savernake MSS). 1 letter from John Brunsden, actor, about his benefit at Plymouth, 1776 (Wilts. RO 9 Savernake MSS). Commonplace book of John Clavel (1603–42) author of *The Soddered Citizen*, covering 1633–

1636 (Wilts. RO 865/502). Minute book of the Marlborough and District Theatre Club 1951–61 (Wilts. RO 810/1). Devizes Amateur Dramatic Society Minute Books 1947–74 3 volumes and other material.

TRURO

235 CORNWALL COUNTY RECORD OFFICE

County Hall, Truro, Cornwall   (0872) 3698

Contact   P. L. Hull, County Archivist

Hours   Monday–Thursday 9–1, 2–5, Friday 9–1, 2–4.30, Saturday 9–12 (except before Bank Holidays) (2 days prior notice required)

Contents   Posters for performances at Truro Theatre (Assembly Rooms) 1789 and 1803, and Falmouth Theatre, 1815 (ref. DD.EN 2417). Some theatre (travelling) posters, mainly for Helston, 19th century (DD.RH). *Journal of a tour into Cornwall*, 1795, (AD 43) describes removable stage at the Assembly Rooms, Truro. Record Office Library contains some printed material relating to Samuel Foote — works and biographies.

TUNBRIDGE WELLS

236 TUNBRIDGE WELLS MUSEUM AND ART GALLERY

Civic Centre, Mount Pleasant, Tunbridge Wells, Kent TN1 1RS
(0892) 26121 Ext. 171

Contact   Miss M. A. V. Gill, Curator

Hours   Weekdays 10–5.30, Saturday 9.30–5. Closed Sundays, Bank Holidays, and Tuesdays after Spring and Summer Bank Holidays

Contents   Sprange Collection: About 180 playbills for the Tunbridge Wells Theatre, (Mrs Baker's Company). October 1794–November 1797; and other misellaneous printers proofs (tickets and notices).
A few miscellaneous 19th century posters, engravings and cartoons. All local.
20th century programmes for the Tunbridge Wells Opera House, and the Assembly Hall.

TWICKENHAM

237A ST. MARY'S COLLEGE. Library

Strawberry Hill, Twickenham, Middlesex TW1 4SX   (01) 892 0051 Ext. 252

Contact   Miss S. F. Kent

Admission   Reference use only

Hours   Term time: Monday–Friday 9–9, Saturday 9.30–12.30
Vacations: Monday–Friday 9–5

Contents   Large collection of texts. Theatre history. 13 drama journals subscribed to and filed.

TWICKENHAM
237B   TWICKENHAM DISTRICT LIBRARY
Garfield Road, Twickenham, Middlesex   (01) 892 0031
Contact   Local Studies Librarian
Hours   Monday–Friday 10–12, 2–6; Tuesday 1–8; Wednesday and Saturday 10–12, 2–5
Contents   Scrapbook of amateur theatre in area, including items relating to Normansfield Theatre and to performances by various members of the Coward family. Album of Edwardian theatrical postcards.

UXBRIDGE
238   HILLINGDON PUBLIC LIBRARIES. Hillingdon Local Collection
22 High Street, Uxbridge UB8 1JN   (0895) 50600
Contact   Mrs C. Cotton, Archivist and Local Studies Librarian
Hours   Monday–Friday 9.30–8, Saturday 9.30–5
Contents   Includes a small collection of Uxbridge playbills and photographs, and Gordon Craig/Ellen Terry material.

WAKEFIELD
239   YORKSHIRE LIBRARIES JOINT MUSIC AND DRAMA SERVICE
c/o Wakefield Metropolitan District Libraries, Balne Lane, Wakefield, West Yorkshire WF2 0DQ   (0924) 71231
Telex   WAKLIB 557330
Contact   Miss A. D. Taylor, Departmental Librarian, Circulation and Special Services
Hours   Monday–Friday 9.30–7, Saturday 9.30–4
Function   The provision of play sets and books about drama and the theatre to educational institutions and independent drama groups in North, West and South Yorkshire. Outside Yorkshire loans are made through the national interlending system.
Contents   57,000 printed texts. 4,000 play sets. 380,000 music scores. Plus a collection of books on the drama and dramatic history.

WAKEFIELD
240   WAKEFIELD MUSEUM
Wood Street, Wakefield, West Yorkshire   (0924) 370211 Ext. 7190
Contact   Gordon Watson
Hours   Monday–Saturday 10.30–12.30, 1.30–5

Contents	Playbills for the Theatre, Wakefield — late 18th and early 19th centuries. Programmes: Opera House and other theatres in Wakefield, late 19th and early 20th centuries (small collection). Programmes for Wakefield Operatic Society 1906–20. Plans of Opera House, Wakefield, 1893, Empire Theatre, Wakefield 1921 alterations, also Wakefield cinemas 1910s and 1920s.
Indexes	Catalogue cards.

WALSALL

241 WALSALL LIBRARY AND MUSEUM SERVICES

Central Library, Lichfield Street, Walsall WS1 1TR   (0922) 21244 Ext. 3111

Contact	Archives Services
Hours	Local Studies Room: Monday 10–7, Tuesday–Friday 9.30–7, Saturday 9.30–5 Archives: Monday 10–7, Tuesday–Friday 9.30–12.30, 1.30–5, Saturday 9.30–12.30 Appointments are obligatory for Saturdays and recommended for weekdays.
Contents	Collection of c.400 theatre and music hall playbills, posters and programmes c.1840+, relating to local theatres, concert halls and church and school concerts.
Indexes	Catalogue of collection arranged by theatre and in chronological order by date of performance.
Note	In the Summer of 1986 the Local History and Archives Collections will move to:- Walsall Local History Centre, Essex Street, Walsall. Hours: Tuesday, Thursday, Friday 9.30–5.30; Wednesday 9.30–7; Saturday 9.30–1.

WALSALL

242 WEST MIDLANDS COLLEGE. The Library

Gorway, Walsall WS1 3BD   (0922) 29141

Contact	C. Evans
Admission	To the public for reference
Hours	Term time: Monday–Thursday 8.30–9, Friday 8.30–4.30, Saturday open a.m., Sunday p.m.
Contents	General collection on film, theatre and drama to meet needs of students.

WARRINGTON

243 NORTH CHESHIRE COLLEGE. Padgate Campus Library

Fearnhead, Warrington, Cheshire WA2 0DB   (0925) 814343

Contact	Miss M. M. Tye

Admission	Open to the public for consultation and study
Hours	Term time: Monday–Thursday 9–8, Friday 9–5, Saturday 1–5 Vacations: Monday–Friday 9–12.30, 1.30–5
Contents	General collection to meet needs of drama and theatre students. Student dissertations include: *A history of the theatre in Liverpool from its origins to the Theatre Royal,* 1971, by Susan Boyle. *The theatre in Stockport,* by W. Brackenbury, 1974. *The Theatre Royal, Barnsley,* by Mary Fairhurst, 1973. *Changes in Birmingham theatre during the late 19th and early 20th centuries,* by Susan Hodgkins, 1973. *The theatre in Warrington,* by W. Barlow and others, 1974. *Theatre in Leigh: aspects of its history,* by R. M. Wright, n.d.

WARRINGTON

244 WARRINGTON PUBLIC LIBRARY
(Cheshire Libraries and Museums)

Museum Street, Warrington, Cheshire WA1 1JB   (0925) 31873

Telex	61355
Contact	Reference Librarian
Hours	Reference Library: Monday–Wednesday, Friday 9–7.30, Thursday 9–5, Saturday 9–1
Contents	Local Collection includes material on: Scotland Road Theatre, Warrington, 1805–1916 — Archive material strong for 1805–1870s. Royal Court Theatre, Warrington, 1861–1957 — Programmes. Palace and Hippodrome Theatres, 1907–1931 (later cinema and variety, now a bingo hall). Red Lion Hotel Music Hall and Concerts, 1784–1860s — Bills and programmes. Music Hall, Bewsey Street, 1834–1840 — Bills and programmes. Music Hall, Market Place, 1791–1862 — Handbills. Old Coffee House, Horse Market Street, 1788–1810. Theatre, Sankey Street, 1881–1893 (Variety and circus). Parr Hall, 1895 — Posters.

WARWICK

245 WARWICK COUNTY RECORD OFFICE

Priory Park, Cape Road, Warwick CV34 4JS   (0926) 49431 Ext. 2508

Contact	M. W. Farr, County Archivist
Hours	Monday–Thursday 9–1, 2–5.30, Friday 9–1, 2–5, Saturday 9–12.30
Contents	A collection of 17th, 18th and early 19th century plays, both printed and MSS; including microfilm of manuscripts in the possession of the Newdigate Family. Archives include licensing records with correspondence relating to theatres in Warwick, Leamington Spa, Ragley and Stratford upon Avon. The Pennant

Papers: Thomas Pennant (1726–98) include playbills and associated documents on Eaton Hall Theatre, the theatre at Wynnstay and performances in Holywell.

WEYMOUTH

246 WEYMOUTH REFERENCE LIBRARY

Westwey Road, Weymouth, Dorset DT4 8SU   (0305) 786498

Contact	Reference Librarian
Hours	Monday, Tuesday, Thursday, Friday 9.30–7, Saturday 9–1. Closed Wednesday
Contents	Theatre Royal, Esplanade, Weymouth: 160 playbills for 1770–1859. Playbills for Theatre Royal, St Nicholas Street, Weymouth 1868, Corn Exchange, Dorchester; Loyalty Theatre, Dorchester and Dorchester Theatre.
Indexes	Chronological list available.

WIGAN

247 WIGAN PUBLIC LIBRARY

Local History Collection, Rodney Street, Wigan WN1 1DQ   (0942) 41387/8

Contact	D. E. Williams, Reference Librarian
Hours	Monday–Friday 9.30–7 except Wednesday 9.30–1, Saturday 10–3.30
Contents	A few programmes and cuttings and photographs of theatres and music halls in the Wigan area.

WINCHESTER

248 HAMPSHIRE RECORD OFFICE

20 Southgate Street, Winchester, Hants SO23 9EF   (0962) 63153/4

Contact	County Archivist
Hours	Monday–Thursday 9–4.45, Friday 9–4.15 April–September: open 2nd and 4th Saturday in month 9–12 October–March: every Saturday 9–12 Appointments must be made for all Saturdays
Contents	Include: Quarter Sessions Order Books contain some references to drama at Romsey, Ryde and Gosport 1813–1830. 10 reports of legal proceedings indexed. Account books of the receipts and payments of the Portsmouth Theatre, for the summer seasons 1771–1774. Pamphlet collection includes texts of a number of 18th century plays. Also playbills and programmes relating to theatres in the county and other venues. Collection also includes accounts of King's Theatre, Haymarket 1716–1717 (15M50/127). Lease of the Theatre, Windsor 1830 (36M68).

WINCHESTER

249 KING ALFRED'S COLLEGE OF HIGHER EDUCATION. Drama Department

Sparkford Road, Winchester SO22 4NR   (0962) 62281

Contact   Dean of Drama, Dr Paul Ranger

Admission   For reference

Hours   Term time: Monday–Thursday 9–8.45, Friday 9–8, Saturday & Sunday 1–5
               Vacations: Monday–Friday 9–4

Contents   A small collection of 18th century plays and contemporary works on performance. A collection of printed plays and material relating to Henry Arthur Jones.

WINCHESTER

250 KING ALFRED'S COLLEGE OF HIGHER EDUCATION. Library

Sparkford Road, Winchester SO22 4NR   (0962) 62281 Ext. 229

Contact   The Librarian

Admission   External readers may use for reference or borrow, depending on reason

Hours   Term time: Monday–Thursday 9–8.45, Friday 9–8, Saturday & Sunday 1–5
               Vacations: Monday–Friday 9–4

Contents   General stock relevant to needs of drama and theatre studies students.

WINCHESTER

251 WINCHESTER CITY MUSEUM

Hyde Historic Resources Centre, 75 Hyde Street, Winchester, Hampshire
                                               (0962) 68166 Ext. 2280

Contacts   Mrs T. Brisbane and Miss K. Parker

Admission   By appointment

Hours   9–5

Contents   Theatre Royal, Winchester: posters 1851–6. Winchester posters dated 1806 and 1836.

WOLVERHAMPTON

252 WOLVERHAMPTON CENTRAL LIBRARY. Reference Department

Snow Hill, Wolverhampton WV1 3AX   (0902) 773824/5/6

Contact   Mrs C. West, Reference Librarian, or Miss E. A. Rees, Archivist

Hours   Monday–Friday 10–7, Saturday 10–5 (by appointment)

Contents   10 photographs relating to the re-opening of the Grand Theatre,
                  Wolverhampton. Large number of programmes from late 19th
                  century (theatre opened 1894). A few photos, also, of Prince of
                  Wales Theatre, Hippodrome Theatre, and Empire Palace Theatre.
                  Records of the Grand Theatre and theatre and cinema licensing
                  plans in Archives Collections. Susan Fletcher: *A history of the Grand
                  Theatre, Wolverhampton,* 1971 (an MSc. thesis).

WORCESTER

253   HEREFORD AND WORCESTER COUNTY LIBRARY

Local Studies Library, City Library, Foregate Street, Worcester WR1 1DT
                                                  (0905) 353366 Ext. 3813

Contact   Worcester City Librarian

Hours   Monday & Friday 9.30-7, Tuesday & Wednesday 9.30-5.30,
                  Saturday 9.30-4, closed Thursday

Contents   100 playbills relating to Worcester theatres — Theatre Royal and
                  Swan Theatre.

WORCESTER

254   WORCESTER CITY MUSEUM

Foregate Street, Worcester   (0905) 25371

Contact   Brian Owen, Deputy Curator

Hours   Monday–Friday 9.30-6, Saturday 9.30-5. Closed Thursday

Contents   Worcester Theatre Royal: Posters and handbills c.1810-1900,
                  Programmes (mainly amateur productions) c.1920-1950.
                  Worcester Swan Theatre: Posters, programmes c.1968+.

Indexes   Accession files only, listing brief details, donors, locations.

WORTHING

255   WORTHING MUSEUM AND ART GALLERY

Chapel Road, Worthing, West Sussex BN11 1HD   (0903) 39999 Ext. 121

Contact   The Curator

Hours   April–September 10-6, October–March 10-5. Closed Sunday

Contents   Programmes, bills, tickets, cuttings, posters and other printed
                  ephemera relating to: New Theatre Royal 1897-1929, Pier
                  Pavilion 1926+, Connaught Theatre 1935-86.

Indexes   Card index.

YORK

256 YORK CENTRAL LIBRARY

North Yorkshire County Library, Museum Street, York YO1 2DS

(0904) 55631

Contact	Reference Librarian
Hours	Monday–Wednesday 9–8, Thursday 9–5.30, Saturday 9–1
Contents	Playbills and programmes 1767 to date (with gaps). Tate Wilkinson's account books 1781–1784. 2 mss volumes.
	Rosenfeld, Sybil. *The York Theatre,* c.1948. Mss. — a detailed history from 1705–1947. The work was commissioned by the Governors of the York Citizen Theatre but never published.
Indexes	Chronological list of plays in two loose-leaf binders.

PART TWO

257–292

THEATRE SOCIETIES AND ASSOCIATIONS PROVIDING INFORMATION SERVICES

Generally these are organisations comprising members, either individual, corporate, or both, who owe their membership to the payment of a subscription, to their interest in and support for the aims of the organisation, and to their need to receive the facilities and services provided.

These organisations usually have neither the financial resources, staff nor wish to provide information services for non-members (though some are prepared to help enquirers if it is at all practicable).

The societies and associations included are those that provide some sort of information service while not having a formal collection of theatre material.

When writing to these societies and associations enclose an A5 stamped and addressed envelope for the reply.

257 ASSOCIATION OF ARTS CENTRES IN SCOTLAND

Braehead, Nether Anguston, Cutler, Aberdeen   (0224) 732112

Hon. Secretary George C. Morrison

Membership Open to Arts Centres, Guilds and Societies in Scotland; there is also an individual membership.

An information service is provided on 'anything pertaining to the arts or arts organisations in Scotland'.

258 The ASSOCIATION OF BRITISH THEATRE TECHNICIANS

4-7 Great Pulteney Street, London W1   (01) 434 3901

The A.B.T.T. is an organisation for those who help the actor in a technical capacity. It covers both technical and administrative aspects of theatre.

Membership Associate membership is available to those interested in the Association's subject field. Senior grades of membership carry entry requirements.

Information Service This is a free service available to anyone but priority is given to members. Enquiries are preferred by telephone. Research will not be undertaken, but help will be given to researchers if time is available. Information resources include personal knowledge and a stock of reference books.

The A.B.T.T. collects and disseminates information in all relevant fields to its members and bodies who consult it. This is done by specialist committees dealing with theatre planning, training, safety, lighting, sound, materials, management etc.

Publications Journals *Sightline* and *ABTT News*. Data sheets and information cards on all aspects covered.

259 BRITISH ACTORS EQUITY ASSOCIATION (Equity)

incorporating the Variety Artistes' Federation

8 Harley Street, London W1N 2AB   (01) 636 6367 and 9311

Equity was formed in 1930 and takes into membership actors, club and circus performers, stage management, theatre designers and directors, dancers, singers and many others in the entertainment industry. Standard contracts laying down minimum terms and conditions have been negotiated in most areas of work and a number of casting agreements with the employers seek to regulate the number of newcomers entering the profession.

There is no formal information service, but enquiries are answered when possible. Services to members includes legal advice.

260 BRITISH ARTS ASSOCIATION

227 Goldhawk Road, London W12 8ER   (01) 743 4378

The Association is primarily a youth training organisation and has a membership of teachers of drama, dancing and singing. It runs classes and refresher courses, and organises theatre competitions. It provides advice on stage training, private teachers etc., and sets qualifying examinations.

Note: Enquiries from non-members cannot be answered over the telephone.

261 BRITISH ASSOCIATION FOR DRAMATHERAPISTS

P.O. Box 98, Kirkbymoorside, York YO6 6EX

Secretary Carol Brown

Services to members 2 journals and a minimum of 4 newsletters annually.

Services/Information to non-members Very limited. Brochure of Dramatherapy (information includes "What is Dramatherapy", "Training Courses", "Useful addresses", "Reading lists" and application form. Training information, membership information.

Reference/Research materials An almost complete set of back issues of the *Dramatherapy Journal.*

Note: School projects cannot be dealt with!

262 BRITISH CENTRE OF THE INTERNATIONAL THEATRE INSTITUTE (I.T.I.)

43 Welbeck Street, London W1M 7NF   (01) 486 6363

Chairman Neville Shulman

Services to members Liaison with I.T.I. and other international theatre organisations worldwide. Assistance with international theatre initiatives.

Services/Information to non-members I.T.I. aims to serve the entire professional theatre community, but membership is preferred. Overseas visitors come to I.T.I. for advice on what/who to see in British Theatre.

Reference/Research materials Small collection for own internal use. Access to the collections of *London Theatre Record* for production information etc.

263 The BRITISH COUNCIL. Drama and Dance Department

11 Portland Place, London W1N 4EJ   (01) 636 6888

The British Council aims to promote an enduring understanding and appreciation of Britain in other countries through cultural, educational and technical cooperation. One of the ways in which the Counil seeks to fulfil this purpose is by the support of tours abroad by established British performers in the fields of drama and dance, administered by its Drama and Dance Department.

The British Council's support for drama and dance tours can take the form of a Guarantee against Loss up to an agreed maximum, or sometimes an outright subsidy is paid (normally for less expensive tours). The Council also occasionally commissions tours for its own particular purposes, taking full financial responsibility for all aspects, including engagement of companies and performers.

The Department has a small collection of reference material and information on touring companies and backup services. It assists visitors to identify organisations which can help them with their research into British theatre.

264 BRITISH FEDERATION OF MUSIC FESTIVALS

Festivals House, 198 Park Lane, Macclesfield, Cheshire   (0625) 28297

The federation aims to co-ordinate activities in the field of amateur competitive festivals of music, many of which include speech and drama, and to disseminate, through the yearbook, information on festivals and adjudicators.

Information is provided on festivals and adjudicators to anyone interested.

Publications Yearbook, which includes lists of festivals and dates, plus adjudicators and teachers.

265 BRITISH MUSIC HALL SOCIETY

J. O. Blake, 51 Lewes Road, North Finchley, London N12 9NH

(01) 445 7847

Secretary Daphne Masterton

Services to members The BHMS has no library as such, but many members have a good collection from which we can usually answer questions. If unable, we sometimes print enquiries in *Call Boy* hoping another reader can help.

Services/Information to non-members "I usually answer their letters/phone queries giving what help I can."

Research/Reference materials Now at the Passmore Edwards Museum.

266 BRITISH PANTOMIME ASSOCIATION

Department of Drama, University of Manchester M13 9PL

(061) 273 3333 Ext. 3608

Services Will answer specific queries relating to the history of pantomime, but cannot provide free reading lists nor answer requests for broad information on pantomime. It aims to serve those who are seriously attempting to gather and interpret information relating to the history and practice of British pantomime.

Contents Includes private collections of Gyles Brandreth, David Mayer and others.

267 BRITISH PUPPET AND MODEL THEATRE GUILD

18 Maple Road, Yeading near Hayes, Middlesex UB4 9LP   (01) 841 4790

Hon. Secretary Gordon Shapley

Services to members Monthly newsletters. Annual magazine. Regional Councillors. Panel of experts. Technical sheets every two months. FREE to membership.

Services/Information to non-members Regional councillors. Panel of experts. Reply to general correspondence.

Reference/Research materials We have an archivist able to assist in certain circumstances.

268 BRITISH THEATRE INSTITUTE
incorporating Drama and Theatre Education Council

Enquiries c/o 61 Surbiton Court, St Andrew's Square, Surbiton KT6 4ED

Founded in 1971, the Institute was set up to promote interest in and the study of British theatre; it is particularly concerned with theatre and drama in education.

Membership Open to individuals and organisations in the U.K. and abroad.

Publications Until it is financially possible to set up an information and referral centre, the above aims are pursued through the publications programme which includes *BTI/DATEC Reports* and *Special Reports,* bibliographies and directories.

Information is given on education and training, and where possible will be given to researchers; help cannot be given with school projects. A stamped addressed envelope should be provided.

269 BRITISH UNIVERSITIES FILM & VIDEO COUNCIL

55 Greek Street, London W1V 5LR   (01) 734 3687

Secretary Rachel Mackenzie

Services to members 1. Information concerning audio-visual materials in higher education, including use of specialised reference library and large collection of catalogues. 2. Publications on specific topics concerned with the use of film and videotape. 3. Viewing, seminar and editing facilities. There are different categories of membership — for further information contact BUFVC. Individuals may subscribe to the Information Service.

Services to non-members Those making regular use of the Council's services are asked to take out membership.

Reference/Research materials Details of approximately 6,000 teaching programmes, including many items on drama, mime, ballet and the theatre are accessible on-line through the HELPIS file, which forms part of the British Library's BLAISE-LINE service. For further information contact Olwen Terris.

The British Universities Film & Video Council holds in its Information Service a card index of over 300 programmes on all aspects of Shakespearean production, performance and critical interpretation. Includes feature length versions of the plays; feature length adaptations and derivatives of Shakespeare plays; dance, musical or operatic versions of the plays together with material covering acting technique, set design, production and theatre history. The Information Service will be pleased to use the index to answer individual enquiries.

270 CONFERENCE OF DRAMA ASSOCIATIONS

8 Dovedale Avenue, Longford, Coventry CV6 7AN   (0203) 667687

Secretary Mary J. Gallagher (Miss)

Services to members Advisory capacity to county drama associations.

Comments Enquiries received and solved — tax enquiries, for addresses and information about organisations.

271 CONSORTIUM FOR DRAMA & MEDIA IN HIGHER EDUCATION

c/o British Universities Film & Video Council, 55 Greek Street,
London W1V 5LR   (01) 734 3687

Chairman Professor Katharine Worth

Hon. Secretary Dr Richard Cave

Services to members Newsletter ×3 per year; Videos for hire; Slide Sets for sale or hire. Conferences & screenings. The objects of the Consortium are to co-ordinate the use and exchange of information on audio-visual materials for the teaching and study of drama and related topics (dance, mime, music etc.) at university or equivalent levels, and to facilitate the production of such materials by members through grants made from the Central Production Fund. The Consortium is also concerned in representing nationally the interests of members in the documentation and availability of audio-visual materials which may be used in the study of drama.

Services/Information to non-members A series of sets of slides with texts on theatre history, *Theatre in Focus* is published with Chadwyck-Healey Ltd. The Administration Department (c/o BUFVC) will try to help general enquiries relating to drama/theatre with special emphasis on educational needs.

Reference/Research material Reference material open to members in the form of videos and slide sets.

272 The EDUCATIONAL DRAMA ASSOCIATION

310 Harborne Park Road, Birmingham B17 0NE

Contact Malcolm Pomroy

Services Information on child drama, natural dance, and theatre for children as outlined by Peter Slade in his book *Child Drama*. All enquiries should be accompanied by a stamped addressed envelope.

273 GUILD OF DRAMA ADJUDICATORS

Court Lodge, 11 Hale Avenue, New Milton, Hants. BH25 6EZ
          (0425) 611883

Secretary Mrs J. Eyre

Services to members Information regarding availability and qualifications of members. This information is sent to Organisers of Drama Festivals, requiring the services of professional adjudicators.

Services to non-members As above.

Comments The organisation sends out Directories each year to Libraries, Educational Establishments, etc. The Directory contains the names of all members of G.O.D.A. and each member has to be accepted at a special Entrance Conference.

274 INTERNATIONAL AMATEUR THEATRE ASSOCIATION, UNITED KINGDOM CENTRE

19 Abbey Park Road, Grimsby DN32 0HJ   (0472) 43424

Secretary Marjorie Havard

Services to members International information, newsletters to members, Associate membership, international tours, exchanges with theatre groups overseas, International Seminars, Workshops, Tours, Conferences for all types of theatre groups.

Services/Information to non-members Responses to their enquiries and advice on where to find the information they want.

Reference/Research materials Collections of International Newsletters and copies of past Annual Reports of U.K. Centre.

275 The LITTLE THEATRE GUILD OF GREAT BRITAIN

19 Abbey Park Road, Grimsby DN32 0HJ   (0472) 43424

Secretary Marjorie Havard

Services to members Conferences / Seminars / Workshops / Newsletters / Exchanges / International Contacts / Regional activities plus National activities.

Services/Information to non-members Assistance with how to form a theatre group, and to control one's own building.

Reference/Research material Only year books. Back copies of Annual Reports covering a year's work in the LTG.

276 NATIONAL COUNCIL FOR DRAMA TRAINING

5 Tavistock Place, London WC1H 9SJ   (01) 387 3650

The NCDT is an independent body financed by its member organisations which include Equity and the major employers of actors. It exists to encourage the highest possible standards of vocational education and training by accrediation of courses.

Services Provision of information on accredited courses, drama training etc.

277 NATIONAL COUNCIL OF THEATRE FOR YOUNG PEOPLE

9 Fitzroy Square, London W1P 6AE   (01) 387 2666

Contact Peggy White

Hours 10–3

Services The Council's function is to advise people where to go for information, workshops, classes, courses and performances.

278 SCOTTISH COMMUNITY DRAMA ASSOCIATION

Saltire House, 13 Atholl Crescent, Edinburgh EH3 8HA   (031) 229 7838

National Administrator Alan Nicol

Services to members 5 libraries — Inverness/Aberdeen/Glasgow/Edinburgh/ Kirkcaldy. Two professional advisers visiting member clubs. Residential and non-residential courses. House magazine 4 times a year.

Services/Information to non-members Access to libraries on application. Courses provided upon request.

Reference/Research material Each library has a technical section and large number of original plays, house magazine, records, festival entries and performance, reviews, new plays.

279 SCOTTISH SOCIETY OF PLAYWRIGHTS

37 Otago Street, Glasgow G12 8JJ   (041) 339 1787

Secretary James Mackison-Cook

Services to members Reduced photocopy rates/script appraisal. The society aims to promote the development and production of theatre writing in Scotland and acts for playwrights in all matters affecting them. Publications include *Scottish Theatre News* Scotland's professional theatre magazine.

Services/Information to non-members Reduced photocopy rates. General information in all aspects of theatre arts.

Reference/Research materials A small library of scripts and access to Scottish Theatre Archive.

Note: Our society welcomes school or youth organisation enquiries to help promote Scottish theatre and develop a wider knowledge of theatre arts to young people.

280 SOCIETY FOR THEATRE RESEARCH

77 Kinnerton Street, London SW1X 8ED

Contact Joint Secretaries

The Society is run on a voluntary basis, organising and encouraging research into the history of theatre and its techniques in Great Britain. It organises a lecture programme and publishes a learned journal, *Theatre Notebook,* three times a year; an annual book and occasional special studies.

Membership Approximately 750 individual members who are mainly amateur or professional theatre historians, corporate members, educational and reference libraries.

Information services The Society has no permanent office or full-time staff, and operates from the homes of its committee members. It will answer postal enquiries from its own members and from the general public, but it will not undertake research. Its information resource is the combined knowledge of its members.

Library This collection of theatre literature was acquired by means of review copies and gifts from members etc. It is in the process of being amalgamated with the Theatre Museum's book collection and is temporarily housed in the University of London Library (162A).

Publications *Theatre Notebook,* monographs.

281   SOCIETY OF AUTHORS

84 Drayton Gardens, London SW10 9SD   (01) 373 6642

The Society of Authors is a large professional association, primarily of writers and translators of books, but also of writers for the theatre, radio and television. It represents the interests of its members and gives them legal and business advice in matters affecting authorship. The League of Dramatists formerly operated under the umbrella of the Society of Authors, but since 1975 has been amalgamated with it. The Society also acts as agent for literary estates of a number of dead authors including Eliot, Forster, Joyce, O'Casey and Shaw.

Membership £50.00 per annum.

Information service This is limited to advice on contracts, and other legal aspects of the work; the Society cannot help with enquiries concerning writing techniques or read scripts. Its information resources include personal knowledge, legal material and files of clippings.

282   SOCIETY OF BRITISH FIGHT DIRECTORS

54 Belsize Park, London NW3   (01) 722 3226 or (01) 435 2281

Society for professional fight directors working in the theatre, television and films. Members of the Society will answer enquiries from the public, although most of their information work is done for the professional theatre and screen.

There is a membership category for non-professional 'friends'. Subscription £2.00 to Penelope Lemant, 87 Redington Road, London NW3.

Publications *The Fight Director* (1973+) published triannually.

283   SOCIETY OF TEACHERS OF SPEECH AND DRAMA

8 Park View, Mill Lane, Bridge, Canterbury CT4 5LN   (0228) 30823
                                                                                                                    (evenings)

Contact Robin Wynyard

Purpose 'To promote the advancement of knowledge, study and practice of speech and dramatic art, in every form, and to protect the professional interests of members'.

Archives kept at S.T.S.D. Resources Centre, Roseries, Monks Horton, Sellindge, Ashford, Kent TN2 6EA. Tel: Sellindge 2138.

Availability 'Membership open to holders of certain diplomas in speech and drama from recognised colleges, to state-qualified teachers holding certain additional specialist diplomas, to lecturers in colleges and universities, and to teachers trained in speech and drama at certain colleges of education. In addition, others may be admitted on the recommendation of two members, but all applications are scrutinised by the Council before admission'.

Information provided for members and to general public requiring details of teachers, classes etc. in a given area.

Membership enquiries to Mr E. D. Shaw, 25 Coningswath Road, Carlton, Nottingham NG4 3SF Tel: (0602) 875135.

Publications: *Speech and Drama,* published 3 times per year. *Newsletter, List of Members,* published annually.

284   SOCIETY OF THEATRE CONSULTANTS

4–7 Great Pulteney Street, London W1R 3DF   (01) 434 3904

Theatre consultants are frequently appointed to assist the client or architect in dealing with the special problems of designing theatres and other buildings for entertainments, or in the conversion or modernisation of existing buildings. The Society of Theatre Consultants represents consultants practising in this way, and aims to maintain standards, assist in the exchange of knowledge and help clients select suitable consultants.

The Society is not an information giving body as such, and exists basically for the purposes outlined above.

285   SOCIETY OF WEST END THEATRE

Bedford Chambers, Covent Garden Piazza, London WC2E 8HQ
(01) 836 3194

Secretary Bob Lacy Thompson

Founded by Sir Charles Wyndham in 1908, the Society of West End Theatre is the Employers' Association representing not only the owners and managers of the 45 West End Theatres but also the major producing managements in the West End.

The Society is the official voice of the West End theatre industry representing members' interests on various external bodies concerning the theatre-going environment and negotiating with all sectors of the industry, such as Equity (the Actors' Union).

Services to members include legal advice, contacts with potential investors or 'Angels', and a collective research programme which is the foundation of the Society's marketing activities.

The SWET Marketing Office actively promotes West End theatre at home and abroad by publishing and distributing literature on all aspects of theatre-going, participating in travel trade promotions, exhibitions, seminars and the operation of several major marketing schemes including: West End theatre tokens, Leicester Square half-price ticket booth, Student standby, *West End Theatre Magazine,* Senior citizens matinee scheme, the *London Theatre Guide, West End Theatre News,* Information leaflets (e.g. Late Night train services for theatregoers, Theatregoers Guide to Restaurants, How to Book Your Theatre Seats).

In addition the Society presents its own annual Awards to the theatre profession: The Laurence Olivier Awards.

Reference/Research material *London Theatre Guides* from 1920 onwards.

286 STAGE MANAGEMENT ASSOCIATION

81 St Mary's Grove, London W4 3LW   (01) 994 5261

The Stage Management Association is a non-union professional association which looks after the interests of its members, who can be anyone working professionally in stage management in Great Britain.

Membership Open to anyone engaged professionally in stage management in the United Kingdom.

Information service The Association operates from the secretary's home, and provides no formal information service, although telephone enquiries are answered when possible. Enquiries from members normally concern work. Enquiries from non-members are usually about the Association itself, or about careers in stage management. The Association's information resources are personal knowledge and contacts with the professional theatre.

Publication A list of members available for new engagements is circulated to managements each month, on request.

287 SUNDAY TIMES NATIONAL STUDENT DRAMA FESTIVAL

20 Lansdowne Road, Muswell Hill, London N10 2AU   (01) 883 4586

Contact Clive Wolfe, director

Services Mounting of the Student Drama Festival. Information on student drama in Britain, copies of unpublished scripts performed at festival. Programmes and newscuttings.

288 THEATRE DESPATCH

P.O. Box 633, London SE7 7HE   (01) 853 0750

Contact Philip Ormand

Admission By appointment

Contents Extensive collection of theatre leaflets and posters for London 1973+. Particularly useful for 'fringe' material.

289 THEATRES ADVISORY COUNCIL

4 Great Pulteney Street, London W1R 3DF   (01) 387 2666

The T.A.C. is an umbrella organisation to which most national theatrical bodies are affiliated. Its main function is to act as the political representative of theatre as a whole in issues such as the preservation of theatre buildings, campaigning for VAT Zero-rating, and by providing back-up information when approaches are made to the Government for financial or legislative aid to the theatre (embracing commercial theatre and the local authority sector, as well as subsidised theatres).

The T.A.C. is not an information-giving body as such; however, it may be able to give information on new theatre projects or the safeguarding of existing theatres, on theatre policy and on theatre attendances, in connection with which it undertakes a periodic U.K. survey.

290 The THEATRES TRUST

10 St Martin's Clourt, St Martin's Lane, London WC2N 4AJ   (01) 836 8591

Director Lord Jenkins of Putney

Services Answers to enquiries about the ownership of theatre buildings, or which theatres have been the subject of planning applications, and where such matters are within our own experience we are pleased to answer questions. It is not possible to assist school projects.

An Annual Report and factual information about the Trust is supplied to anyone who asks for it.

Reference/Research materials Only the usual Theatre Directories and copies of similar publications.

291 THEATRICAL TRADERS ASSOCIATION LTD.

21–23 York Street, Twickenham, Middlesex   (01) 892 6245

This is a trade association of companies in the U.K. who supply scenery, costumes, curtains, lighting, sound, advertising, printing, make-up, props, etc. for sale or hire for professional and amateur theatre productions, and the entertainment industry generally.

Information is provided on the supplies and services relating to members' products.

292 UNION INTERNATIONALE DE LA MARIONNETTE (UNIMA)

c/o 16 Templeton Road, London N15

Hon. Secretary Written enquiries to Hon. Secretary: Percy Press II

Services to members Activity of UNIMA in furtherance of its aims. The organisation of conferences, festivals, exhibitions, lecture courses and schools, scholarships for young puppeteers, tours and other activities, either directly or by granting patronage. Publications of magazines, recorded material, documents of diverse kinds for information of members. Setting up of collections of varying type for reference. Promotion of international exchanges. Devising of publicity for puppet theatre in the press and other channels. Participating in the work of other associations having similar aims.

Specific queries can be answered **if return postage is enclosed** with enquiries and the replay does not require great length.

Reference/Research material (The Theatre Museum, when at last open, will include some information on UNIMA within the Collection of the British Puppet and Model Theatre Guild.) We can be of little help to 'school project' enquiries beyond sending them a copy of our brochure — **if they send return postage.**

INDEX TO COLLECTIONS

This index excludes collections, libraries and museums whose names begin with the name of the town under which they are listed in Section One.

SUBJECT INDEX

This is an index to the theatres, people and activities mentioned in the entries. It is NOT an index to the contents of the collections. Theatres are not indexed when the material relating to them is in a local collection; for this material turn directly to the appropriate town in Section One.